OF THE ELE

			3A	4A	5A	6A	7A	8A
								2 **He** Helium
			5 **B** Boron	6 **C** Carbon	7 **N** Nitrogen	8 **O** Oxygen	9 **F** Fluorine	10 **Ne** Neon
	1B	2B	13 **Al** Aluminum	14 **Si** Silicon	15 **P** Phosphorus	16 **S** Sulfur	17 **Cl** Chlorine	18 **Ar** Argon
28 **Ni** Nickel	29 **Cu** Copper	30 **Zn** Zinc	31 **Ga** Gallium	32 **Ge** Germanium	33 **As** Arsenic	34 **Se** Selenium	35 **Br** Bromine	36 **Kr** Krypton
46 **Pd** Palladium	47 **Ag** Silver	48 **Cd** Cadmium	49 **In** Indium	50 **Sn** Tin	51 **Sb** Antimony	52 **Te** Tellurium	53 **I** Iodine	54 **Xe** Xenon
78 **Pt** Platinum	79 **Au** Gold	80 **Hg** Mercury	81 **Tl** Thallium	82 **Pb** Lead	83 **Bi** Bismuth	84 **Po** Polonium	85 **At** Astatine	86 **Rn** Radon
110 **Ds** Hassdatium	111 **Rg** Roentgenium	112 **Cn** Copernicium	113 **Uut** Ununtrium	114 **Fl** Flerovium	115 **Uup** Ununpentium	116 **Lv** Livermorium	117 **Uus** Ununseptium	118 **Uuo** Ununoctium

63 **Eu** Europium	64 **Gd** Gadolinium	65 **Tb** Terbium	66 **Dy** Dysprosium	67 **Ho** Holmium	68 **Er** Erbium	69 **Tm** Thulium	70 **Yb** Ytterbium	71 **Lu** Lutetium
95 **Am** Americium	96 **Cm** Curium	97 **Bk** Berkelium	98 **Cf** Californium	99 **Es** Einsteinium	100 **Fm** Fermium	101 **Md** Mendelevium	102 **No** Nobelium	103 **Lr** Lawrencium

© 2021 Sunbird Books, an imprint of Phoenix International Publications, Inc.
8501 West Higgins Road   59 Gloucester Place
Chicago, Illinois 60631   London W1U 8JJ

www.sunbirdkidsbooks.com

Sunbird Books and the colophon are trademarks of Phoenix International Publications, Inc.

Library of Congress Control Number: 2020943537

ISBN: 978-1-5037-5293-1 Printed in China

The art for this book was created digitally. Text set in Scotty O.

IT'S HER STORY

MARIE CURIE

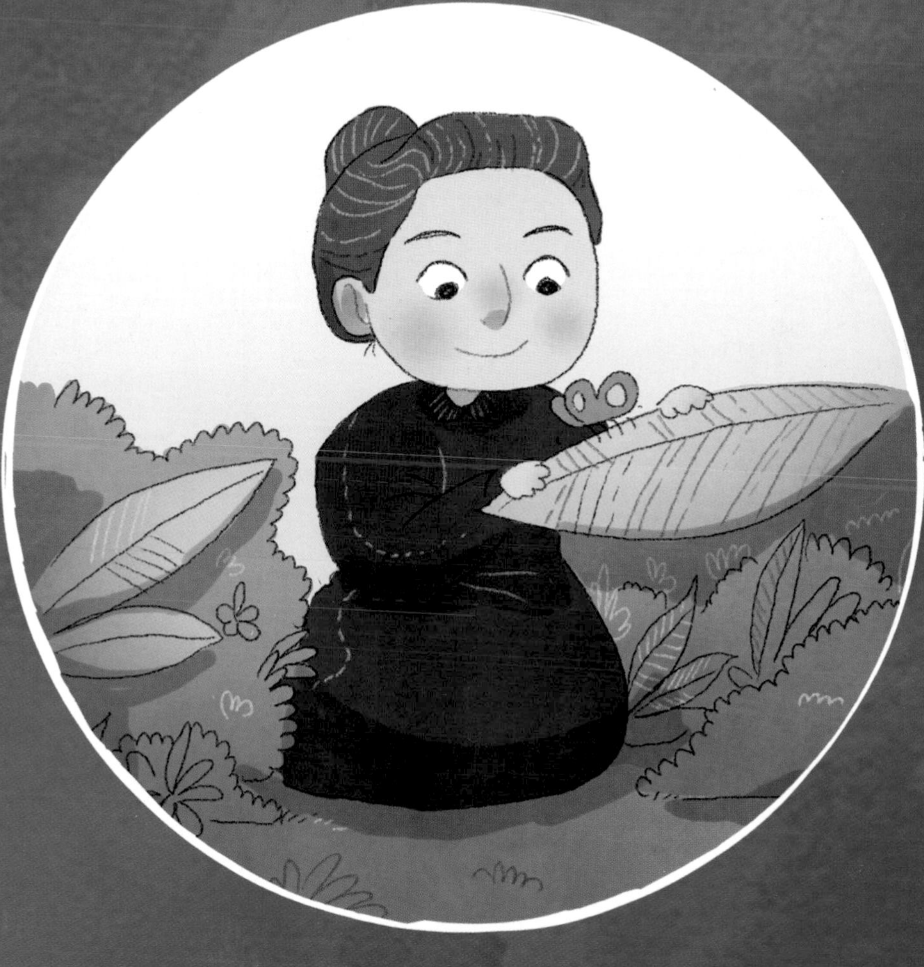

Written by Kaara Kallen
Illustrated by Rosie Baker

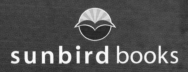

sunbird books

Marie Curie is one of the most famous and honored scientists of all time. She was the first woman in the world to win a Nobel Prize. And she was the first person—man or woman—to win TWO Nobel Prizes.

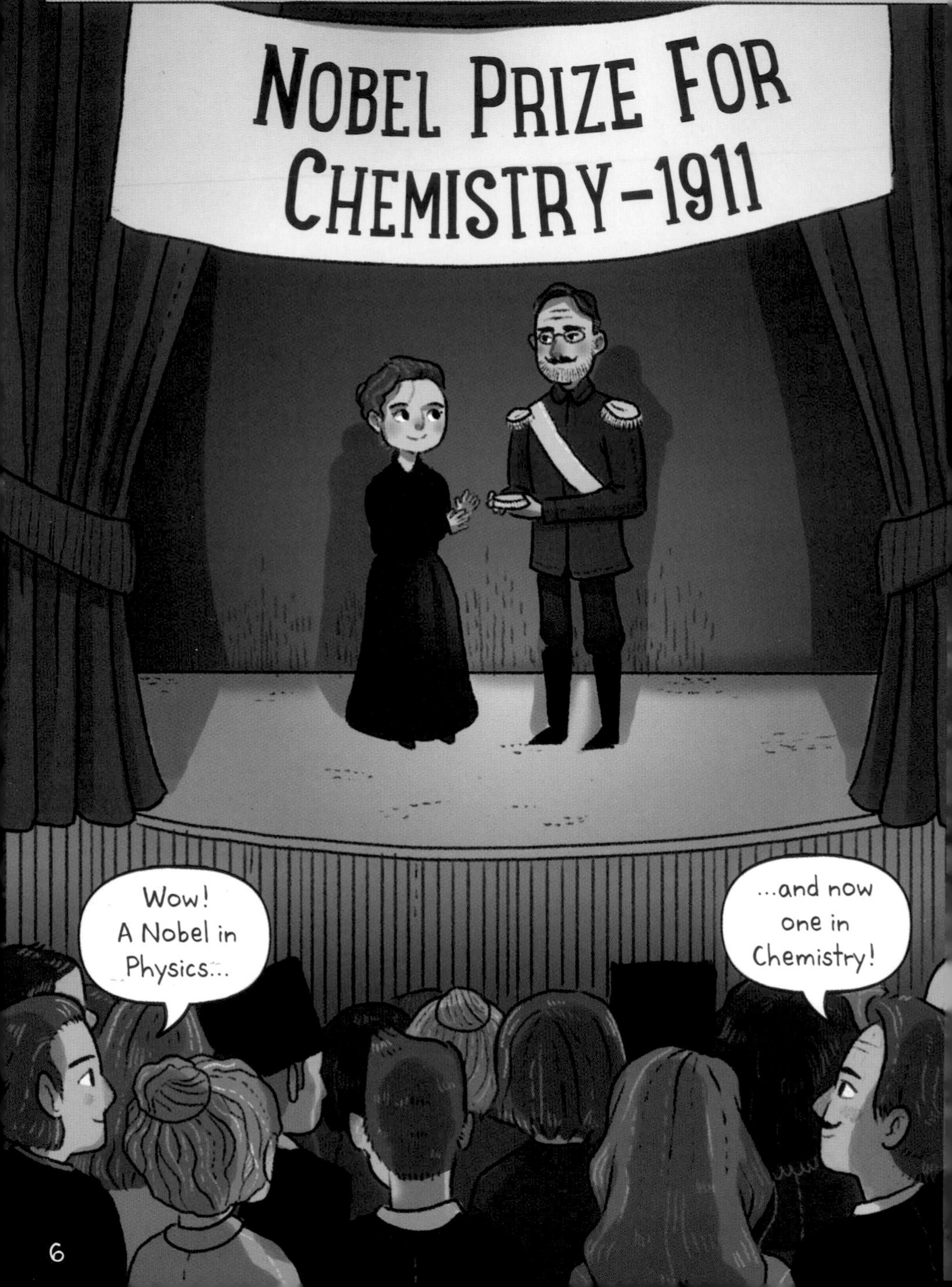
NOBEL PRIZE FOR CHEMISTRY-1911
Wow! A Nobel in Physics...
...and now one in Chemistry!

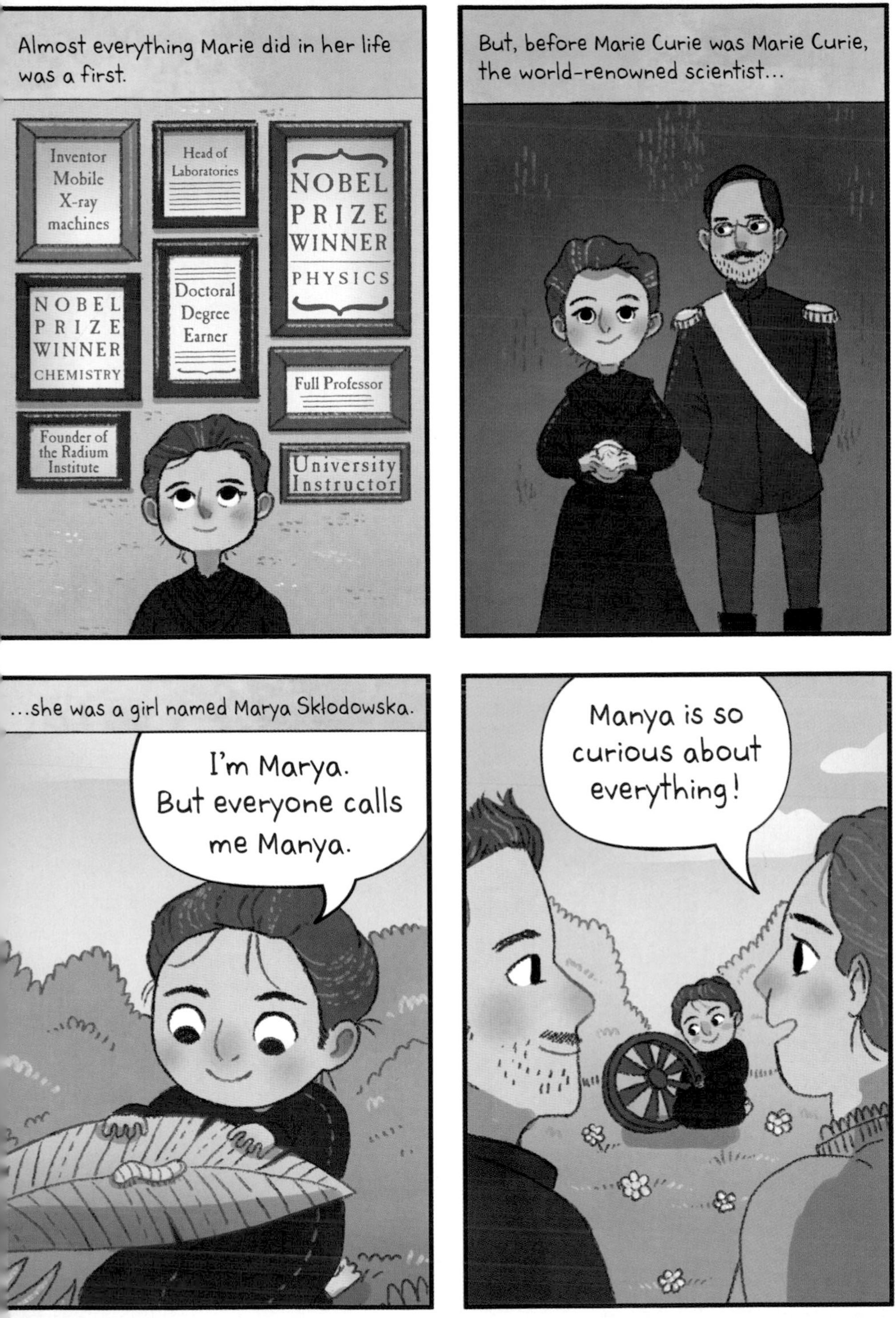
Almost everything Marie did in her life was a first.
Inventor Mobile X-ray machines
Head of Laboratories
NOBEL PRIZE WINNER PHYSICS
NOBEL PRIZE WINNER CHEMISTRY
Doctoral Degree Earner
Full Professor
Founder of the Radium Institute
University Instructor
But, before Marie Curie was Marie Curie, the world-renowned scientist...
...she was a girl named Marya Skłodowska.
I'm Marya. But everyone calls me Manya.
Manya is so curious about everything!

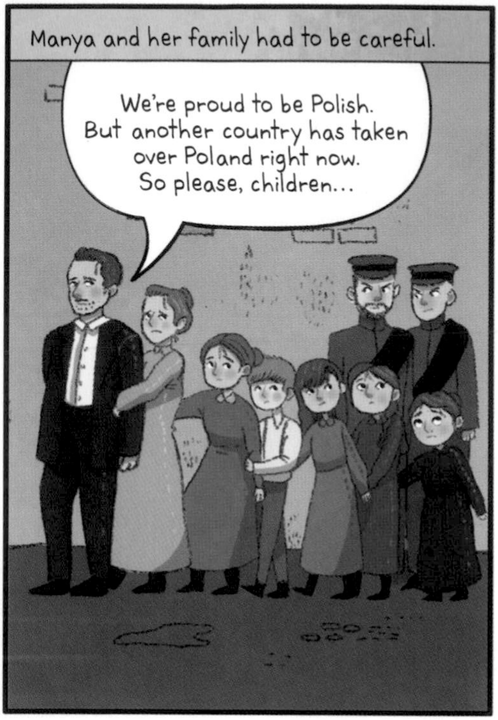
Manya and her family had to be careful.
We're proud to be Polish. But another country has taken over Poland right now. So please, children...

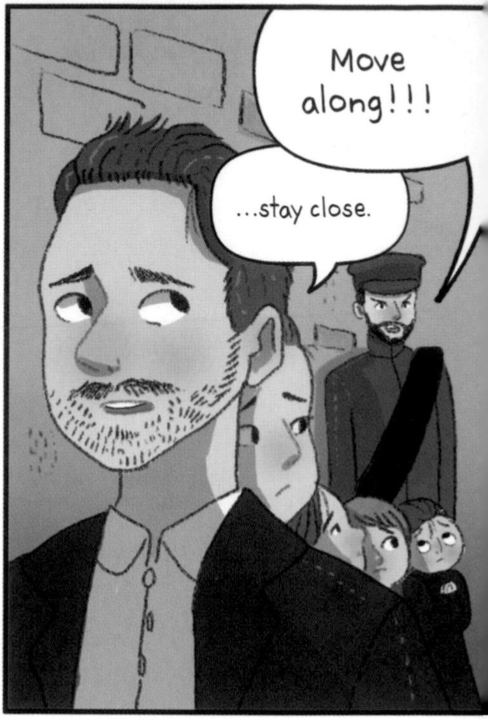
...stay close.
Move along!!!

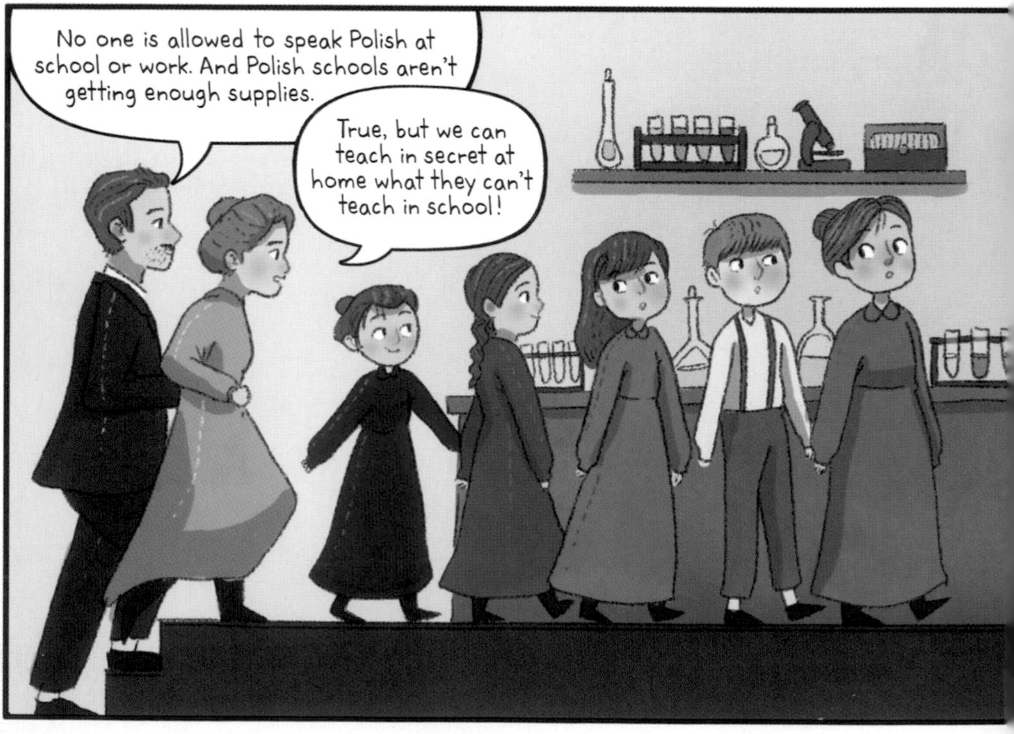
No one is allowed to speak Polish at school or work. And Polish schools aren't getting enough supplies.
True, but we can teach in secret at home what they can't teach in school!

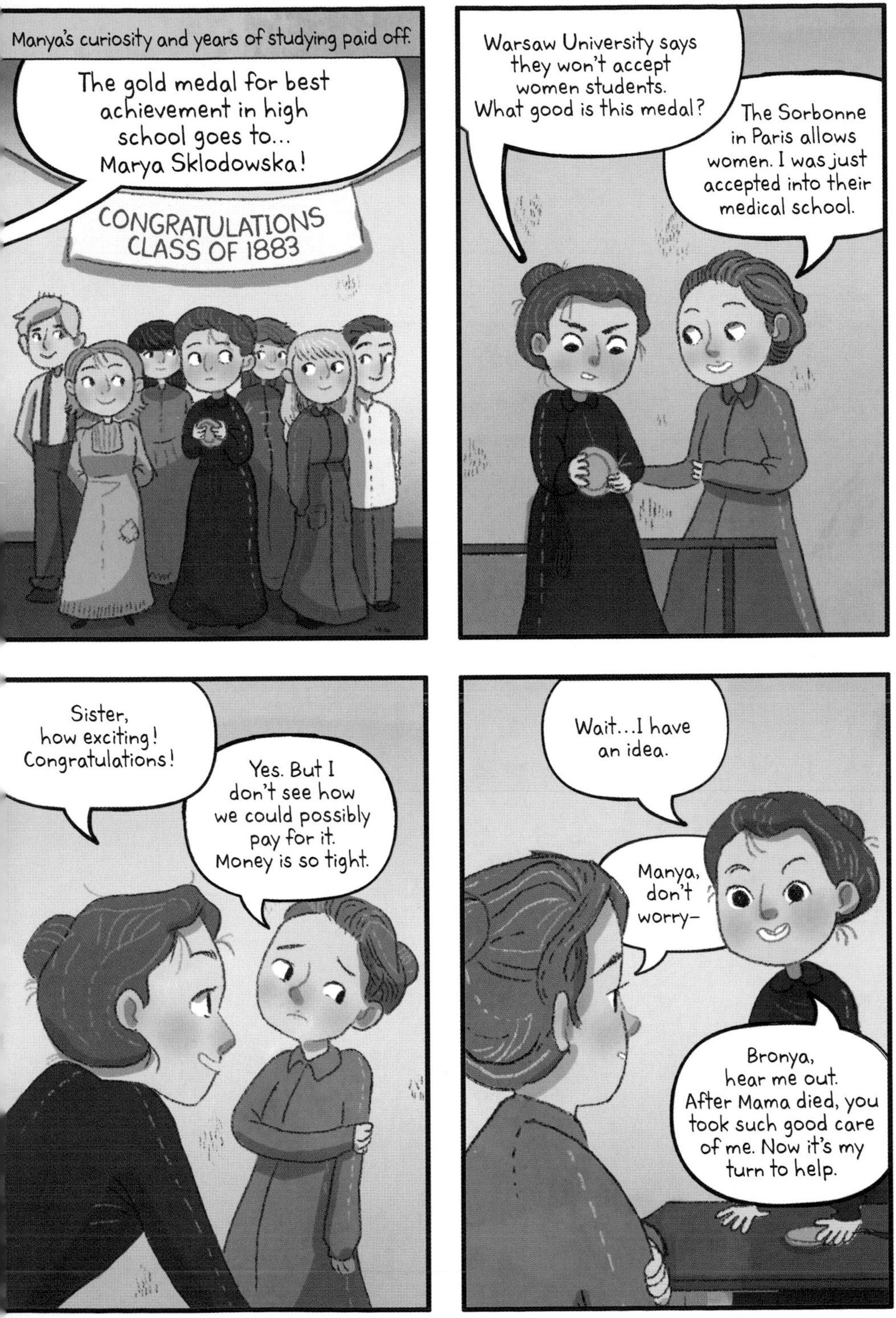
Manya's curiosity and years of studying paid off.
The gold medal for best achievement in high school goes to... Marya Sklodowska!
CONGRATULATIONS CLASS OF 1883
Warsaw University says they won't accept women students. What good is this medal?
The Sorbonne in Paris allows women. I was just accepted into their medical school.
Sister, how exciting! Congratulations!
Yes. But I don't see how we could possibly pay for it. Money is so tight.
Wait...I have an idea.
Manya, don't worry–
Bronya, hear me out. After Mama died, you took such good care of me. Now it's my turn to help.

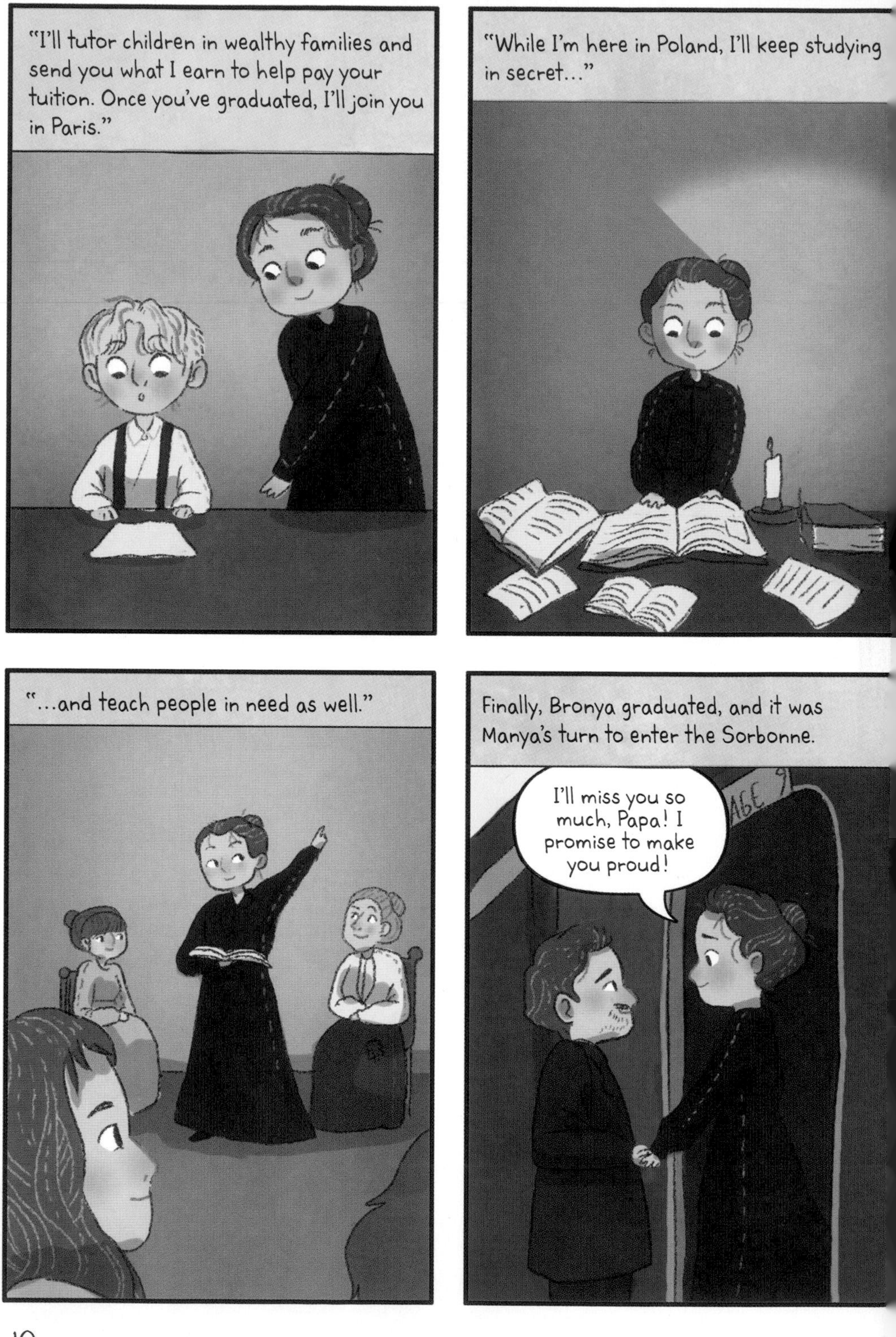
"I'll tutor children in wealthy families and send you what I earn to help pay your tuition. Once you've graduated, I'll join you in Paris."
"While I'm here in Poland, I'll keep studying in secret..."
"...and teach people in need as well."
Finally, Bronya graduated, and it was Manya's turn to enter the Sorbonne.
I'll miss you so much, Papa! I promise to make you proud!

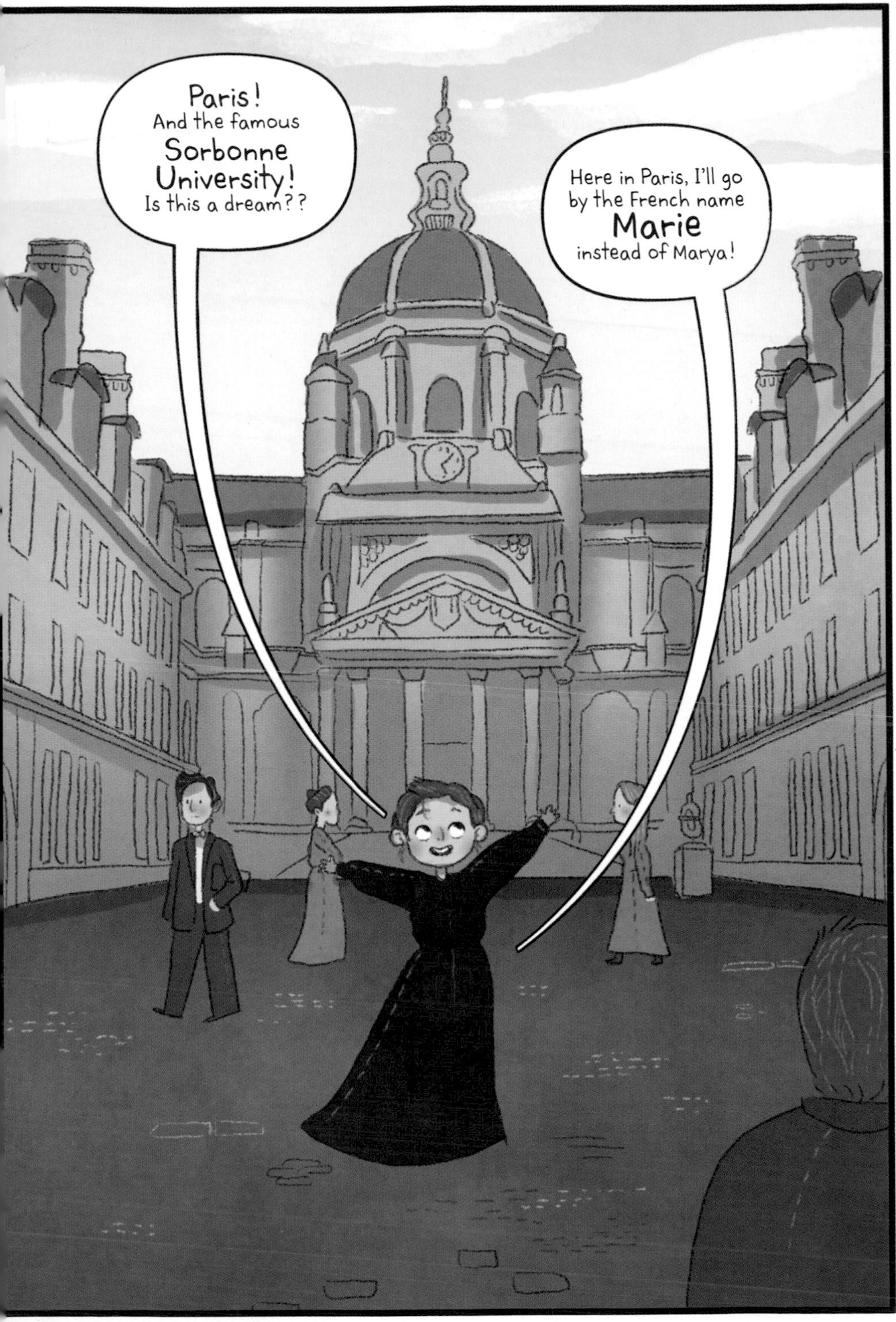
Paris! And the famous Sorbonne University! Is this a dream??
Here in Paris, I'll go by the French name Marie instead of Marya!

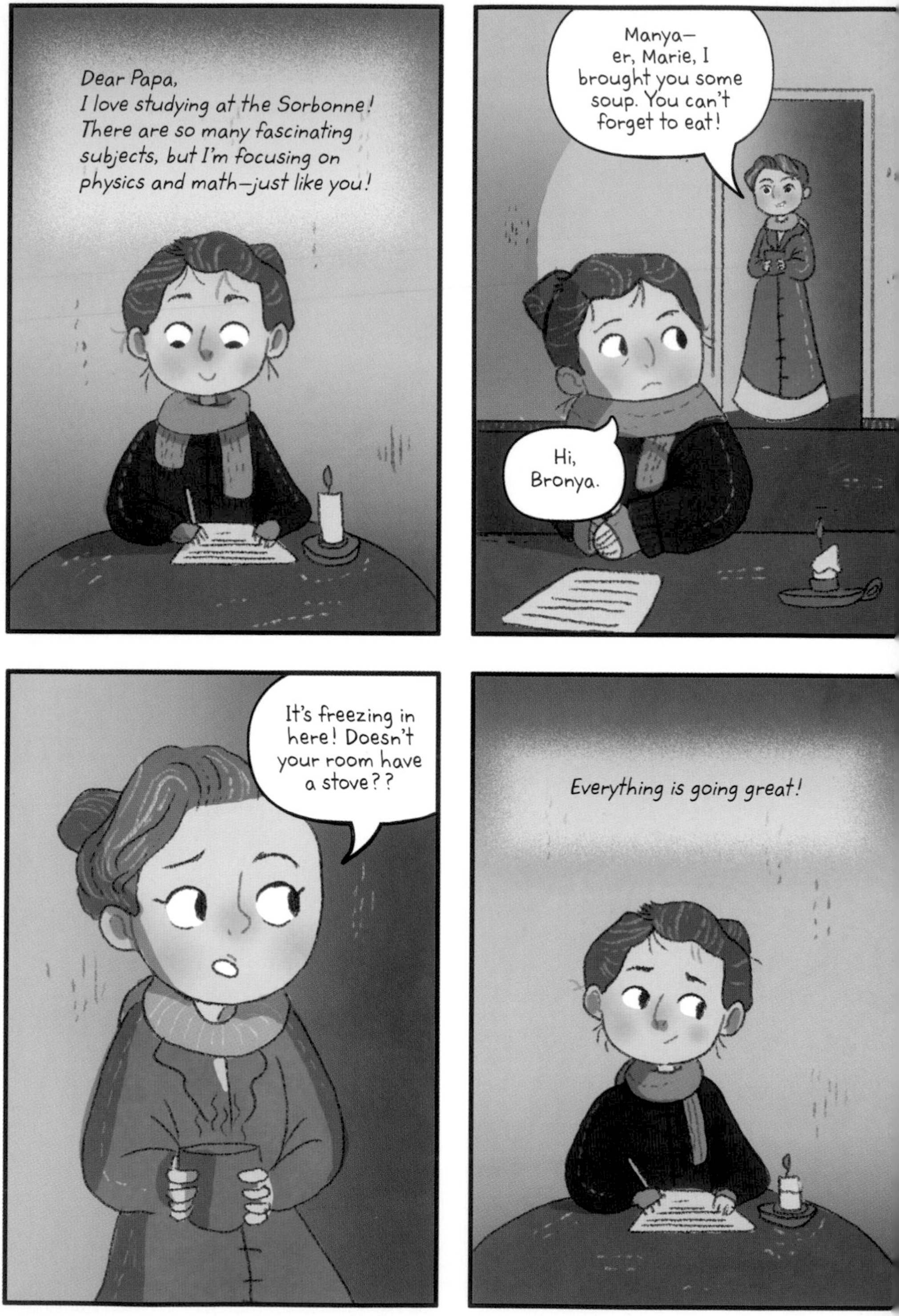
Dear Papa,
I love studying at the Sorbonne! There are so many fascinating subjects, but I'm focusing on physics and math—just like you!
Manya—er, Marie, I brought you some soup. You can't forget to eat!
Hi, Bronya.
It's freezing in here! Doesn't your room have a stove??
Everything is going great!

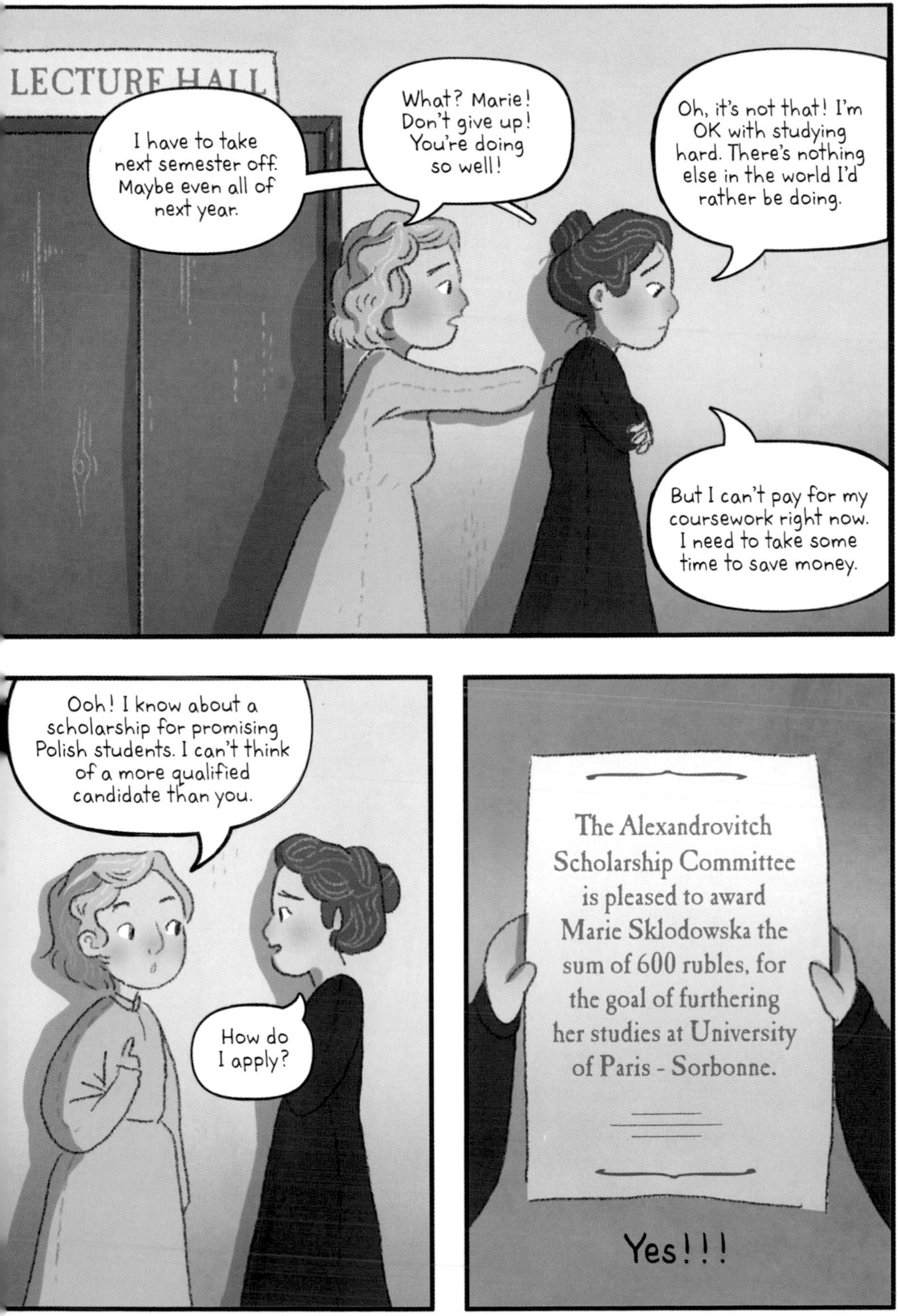
LECTURE HALL
I have to take next semester off. Maybe even all of next year.
What? Marie! Don't give up! You're doing so well!
Oh, it's not that! I'm OK with studying hard. There's nothing else in the world I'd rather be doing.
But I can't pay for my coursework right now. I need to take some time to save money.
Ooh! I know about a scholarship for promising Polish students. I can't think of a more qualified candidate than you.
How do I apply?
The Alexandrovitch Scholarship Committee is pleased to award Marie Sklodowska the sum of 600 rubles, for the goal of furthering her studies at University of Paris - Sorbonne.
Yes!!!

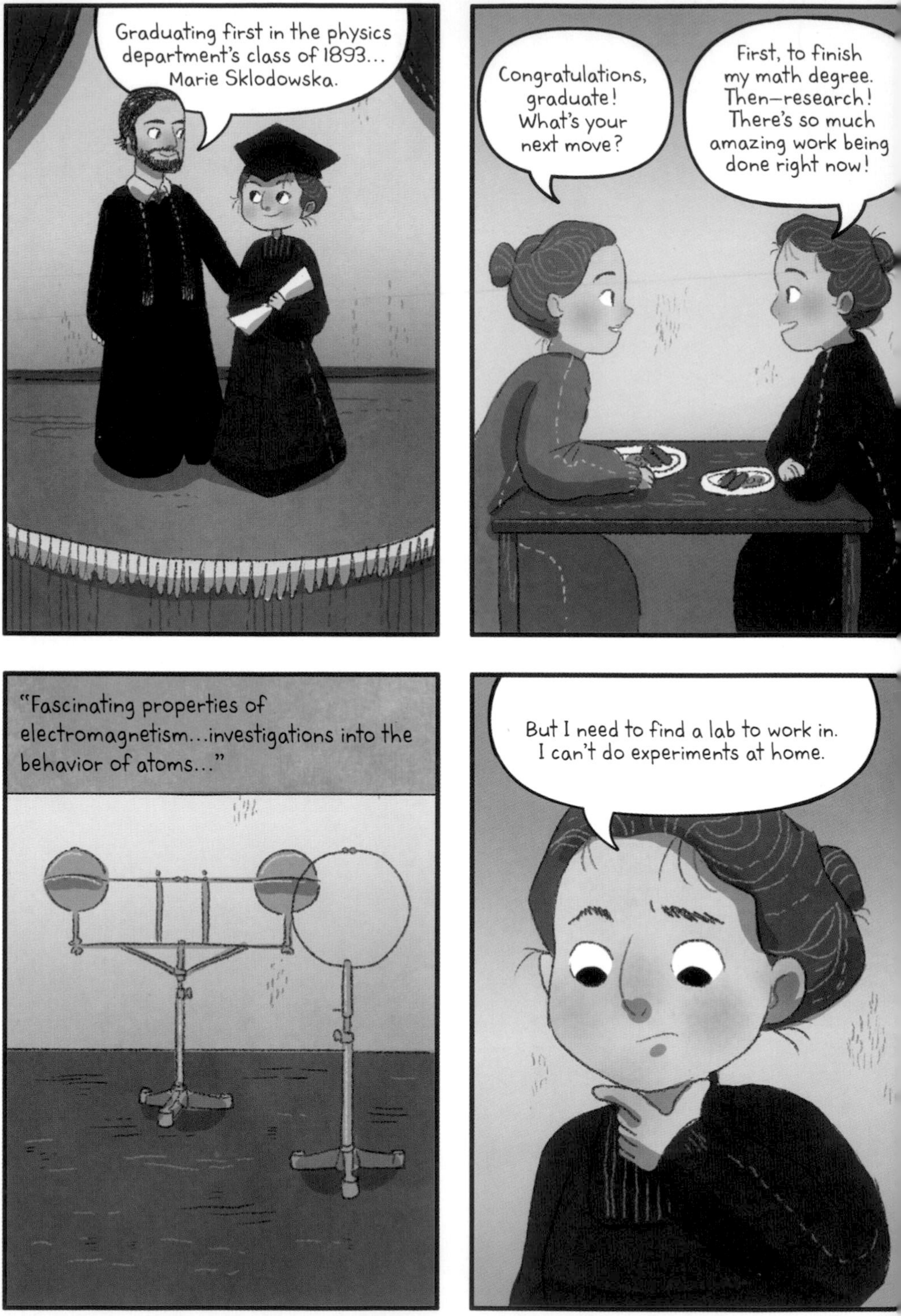
Graduating first in the physics department's class of 1893... Marie Sklodowska.
Congratulations, graduate! What's your next move?
First, to finish my math degree. Then—research! There's so much amazing work being done right now!
"Fascinating properties of electromagnetism...investigations into the behavior of atoms..."
But I need to find a lab to work in. I can't do experiments at home.

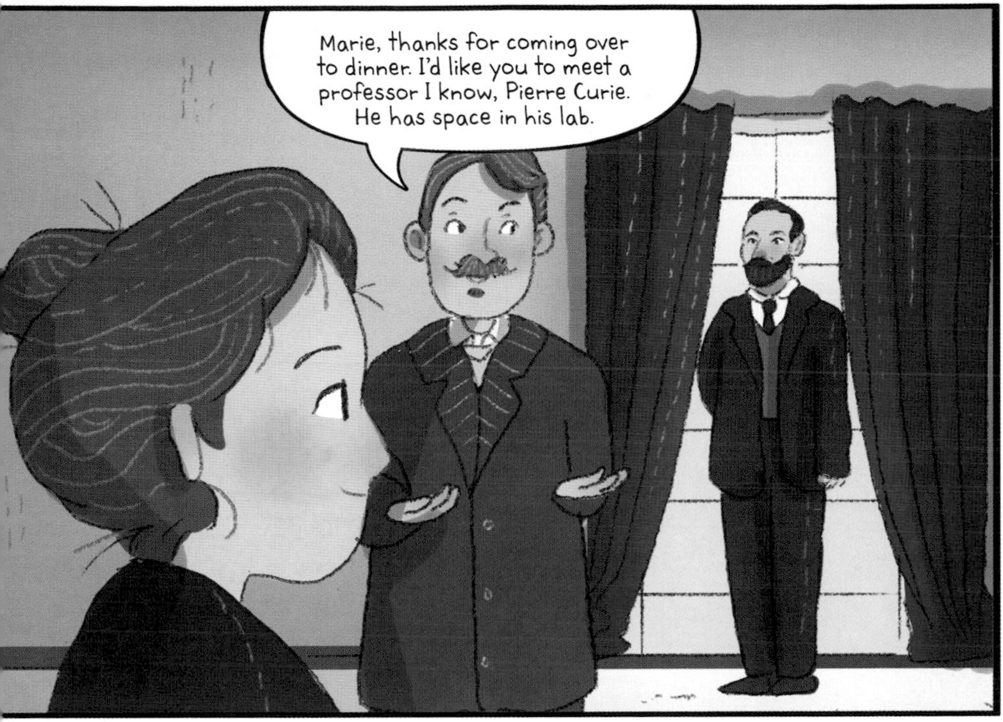
Marie, thanks for coming over to dinner. I'd like you to meet a professor I know, Pierre Curie. He has space in his lab.

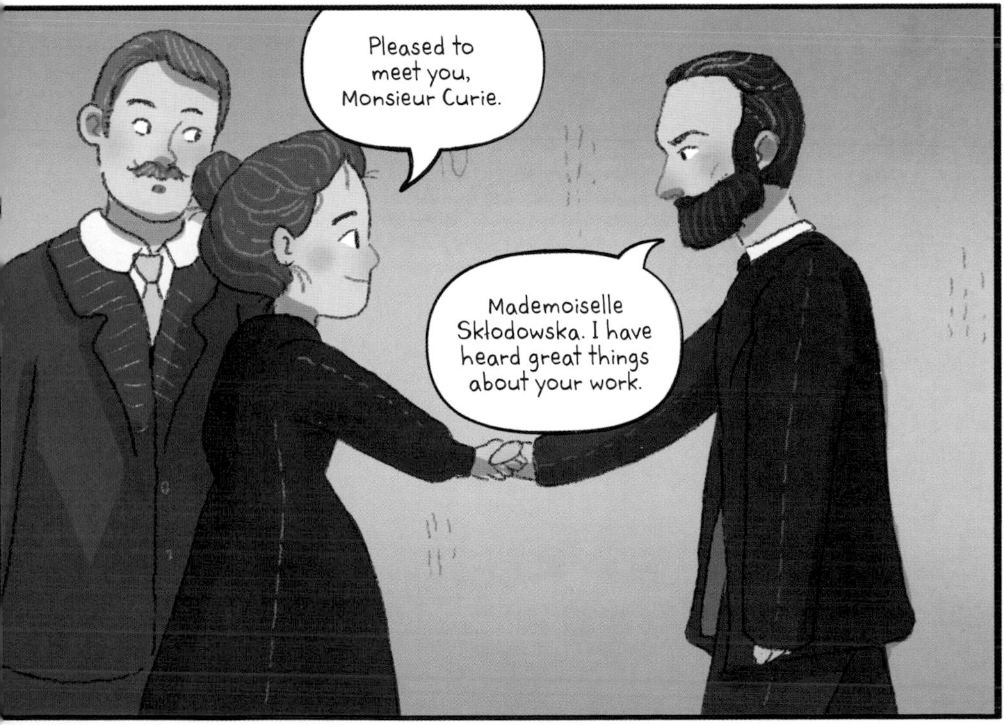
Pleased to meet you, Monsieur Curie.
Mademoiselle Skłodowska. I have heard great things about your work.

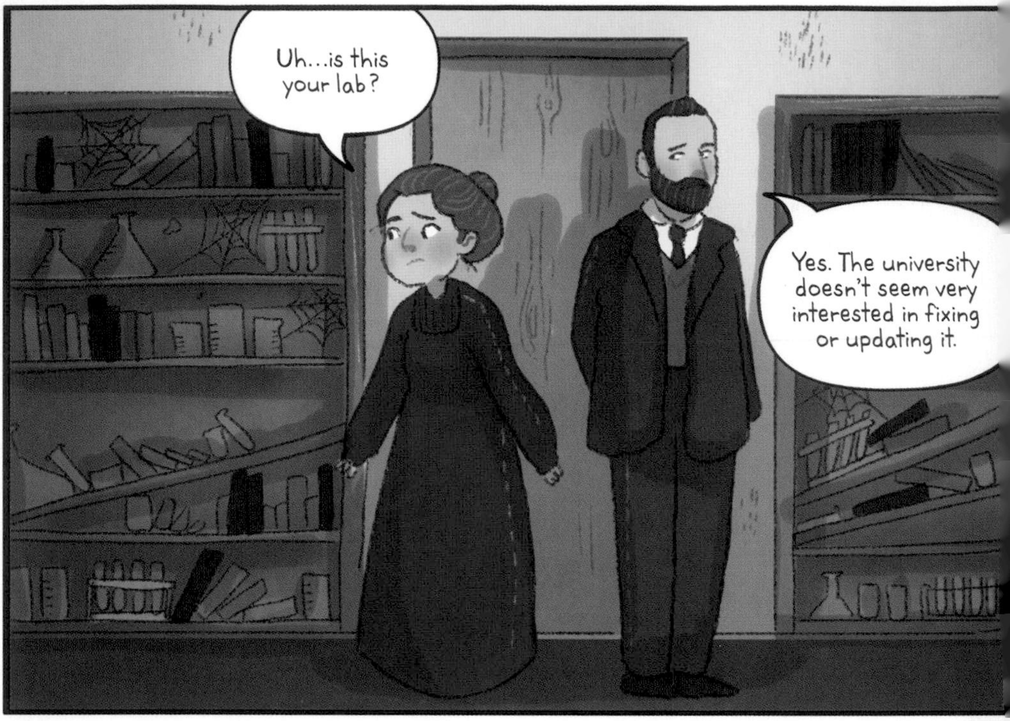
Uh...is this your lab?
Yes. The university doesn't seem very interested in fixing or updating it.

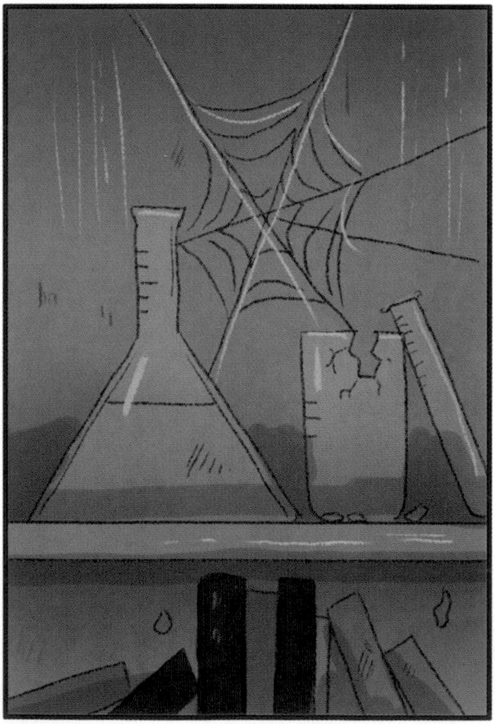

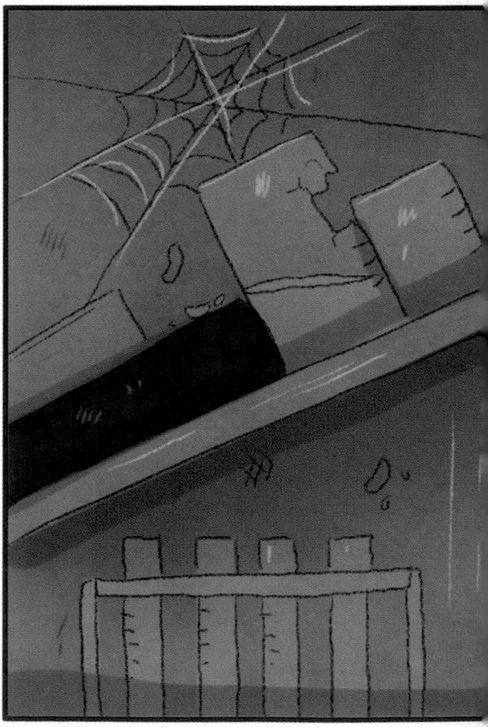

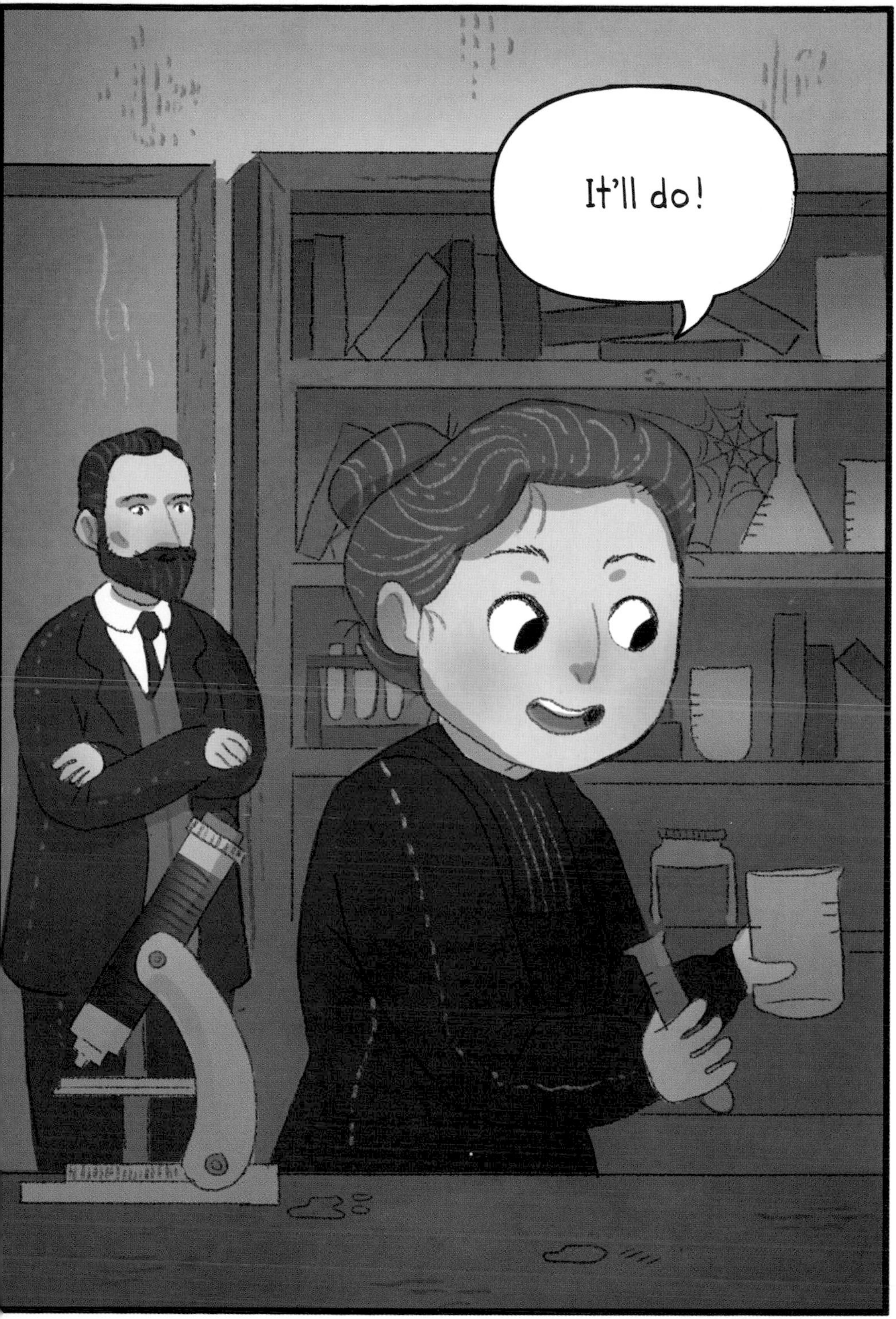
It'll do!

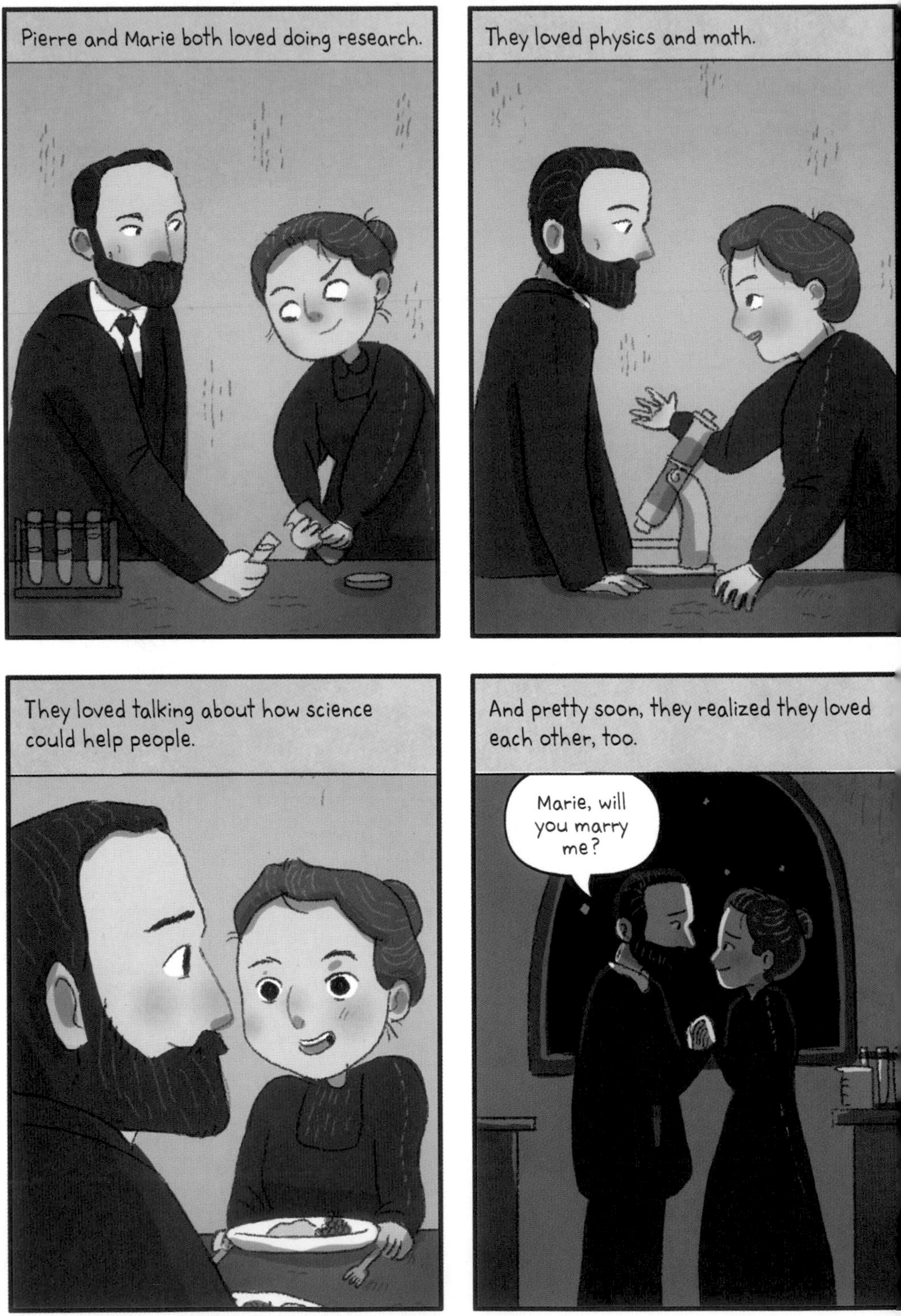
Pierre and Marie both loved doing research.
They loved physics and math.
They loved talking about how science could help people.
And pretty soon, they realized they loved each other, too.
Marie, will you marry me?

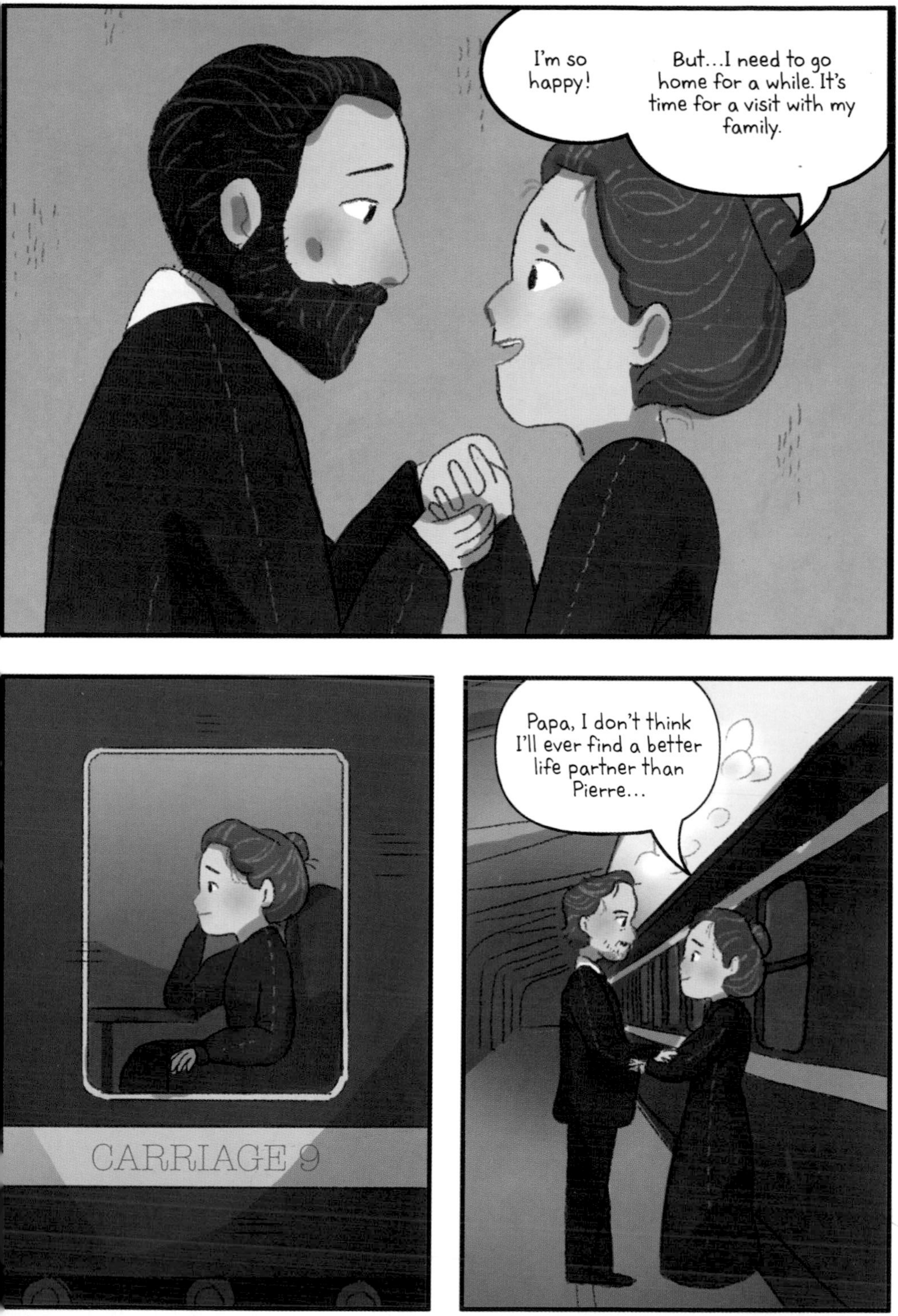
I'm so happy!
But...I need to go home for a while. It's time for a visit with my family.
CARRIAGE 9
Papa, I don't think I'll ever find a better life partner than Pierre...

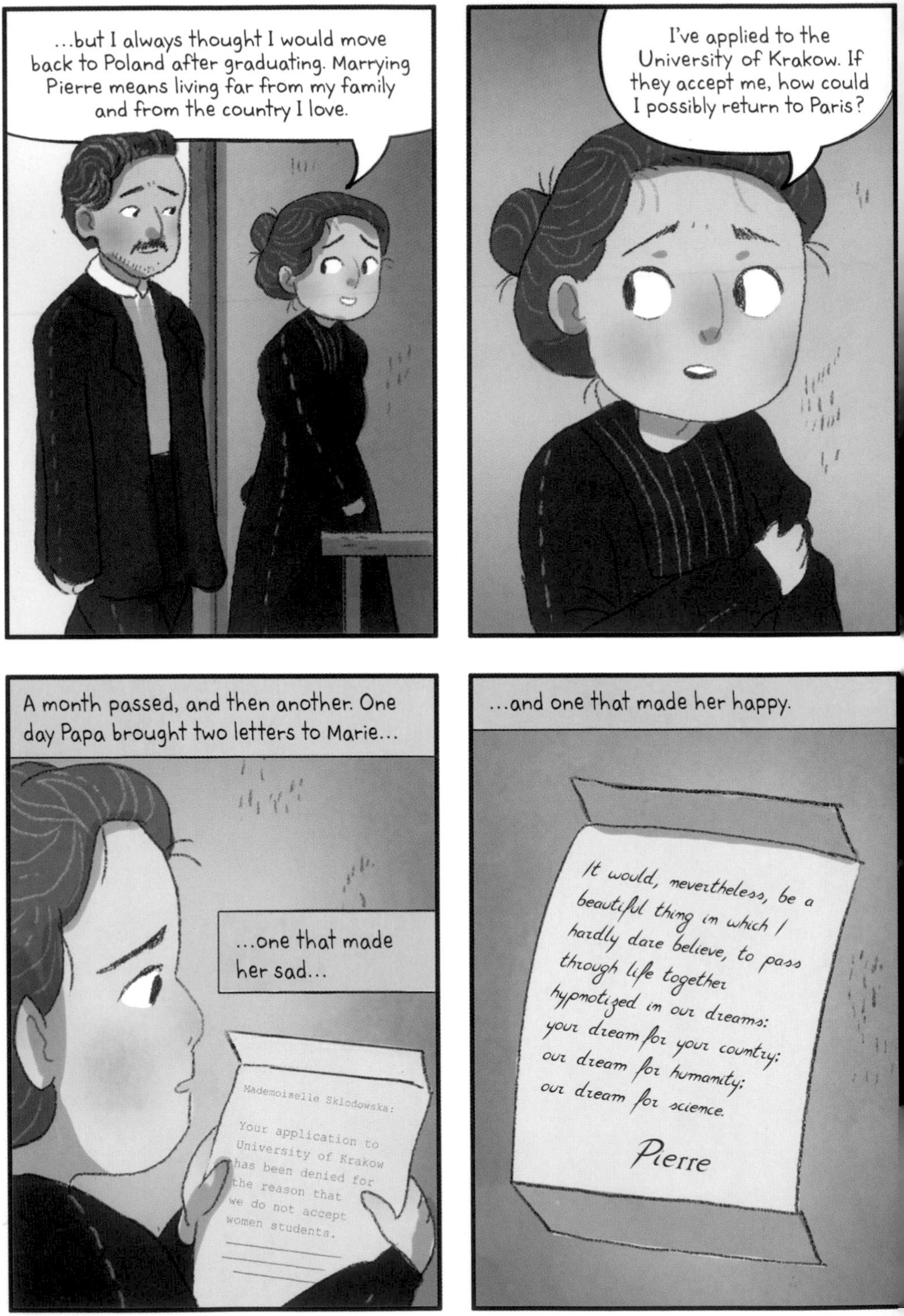
...but I always thought I would move back to Poland after graduating. Marrying Pierre means living far from my family and from the country I love.
I've applied to the University of Krakow. If they accept me, how could I possibly return to Paris?
A month passed, and then another. One day Papa brought two letters to Marie...
...one that made her sad...
Mademoiselle Sklodowska:
Your application to University of Krakow has been denied for the reason that we do not accept women students.
...and one that made her happy.
It would, nevertheless, be a beautiful thing in which I hardly dare believe, to pass through life together hypnotized in our dreams: your dream for your country; our dream for humanity; our dream for science.
Pierre

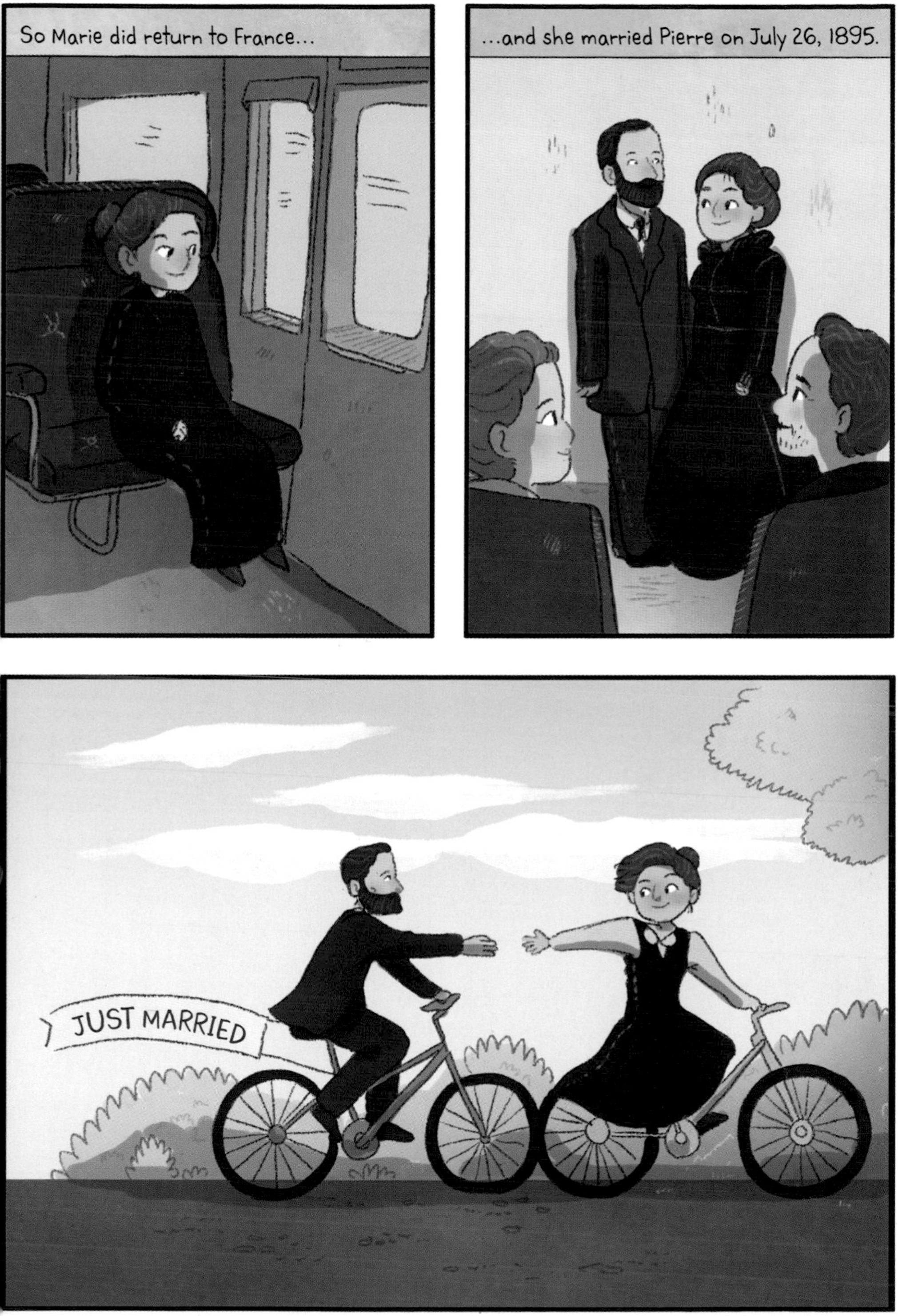
So Marie did return to France...
...and she married Pierre on July 26, 1895.
JUST MARRIED

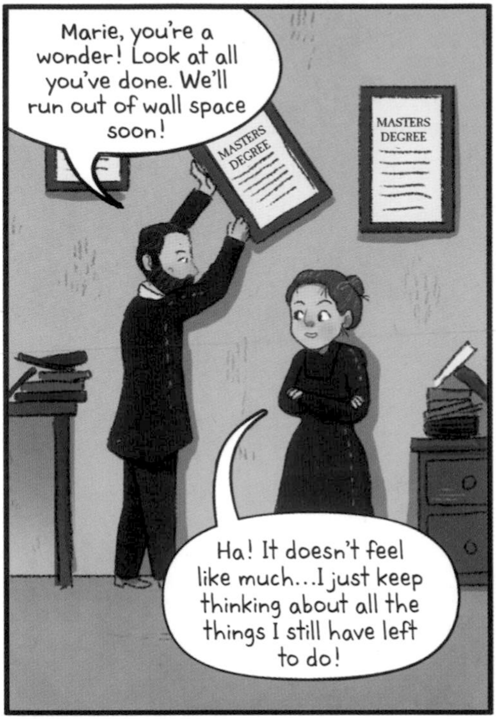
Marie, you're a wonder! Look at all you've done. We'll run out of wall space soon!
MASTERS DEGREE
MASTERS DEGREE
Ha! It doesn't feel like much...I just keep thinking about all the things I still have left to do!

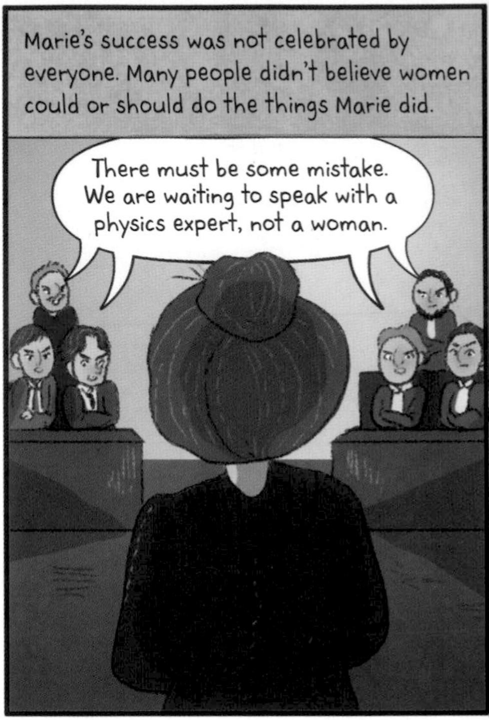
Marie's success was not celebrated by everyone. Many people didn't believe women could or should do the things Marie did.
There must be some mistake. We are waiting to speak with a physics expert, not a woman.

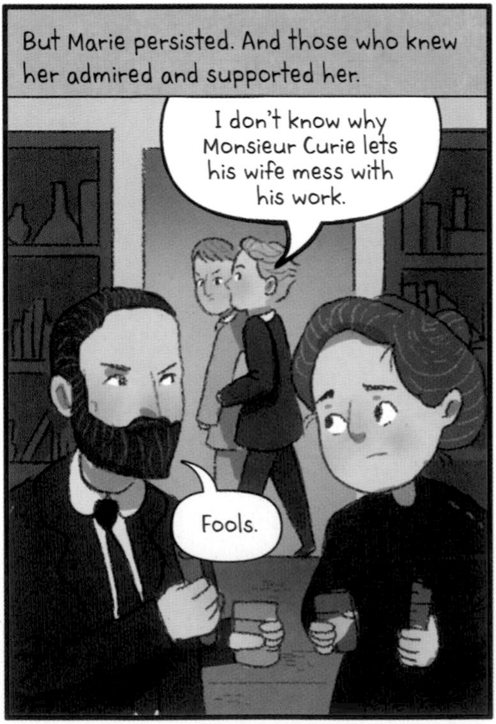
But Marie persisted. And those who knew her admired and supported her.
I don't know why Monsieur Curie lets his wife mess with his work.
Fools.

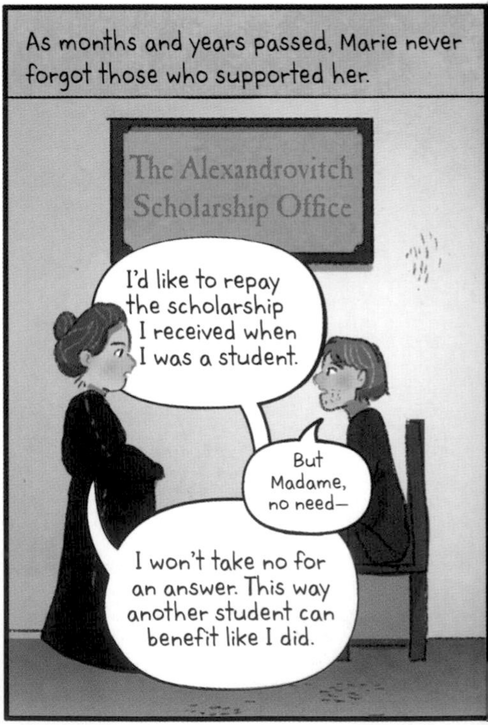
As months and years passed, Marie never forgot those who supported her.
The Alexandrovitch Scholarship Office
I'd like to repay the scholarship I received when I was a student.
But Madame, no need—
I won't take no for an answer. This way another student can benefit like I did.

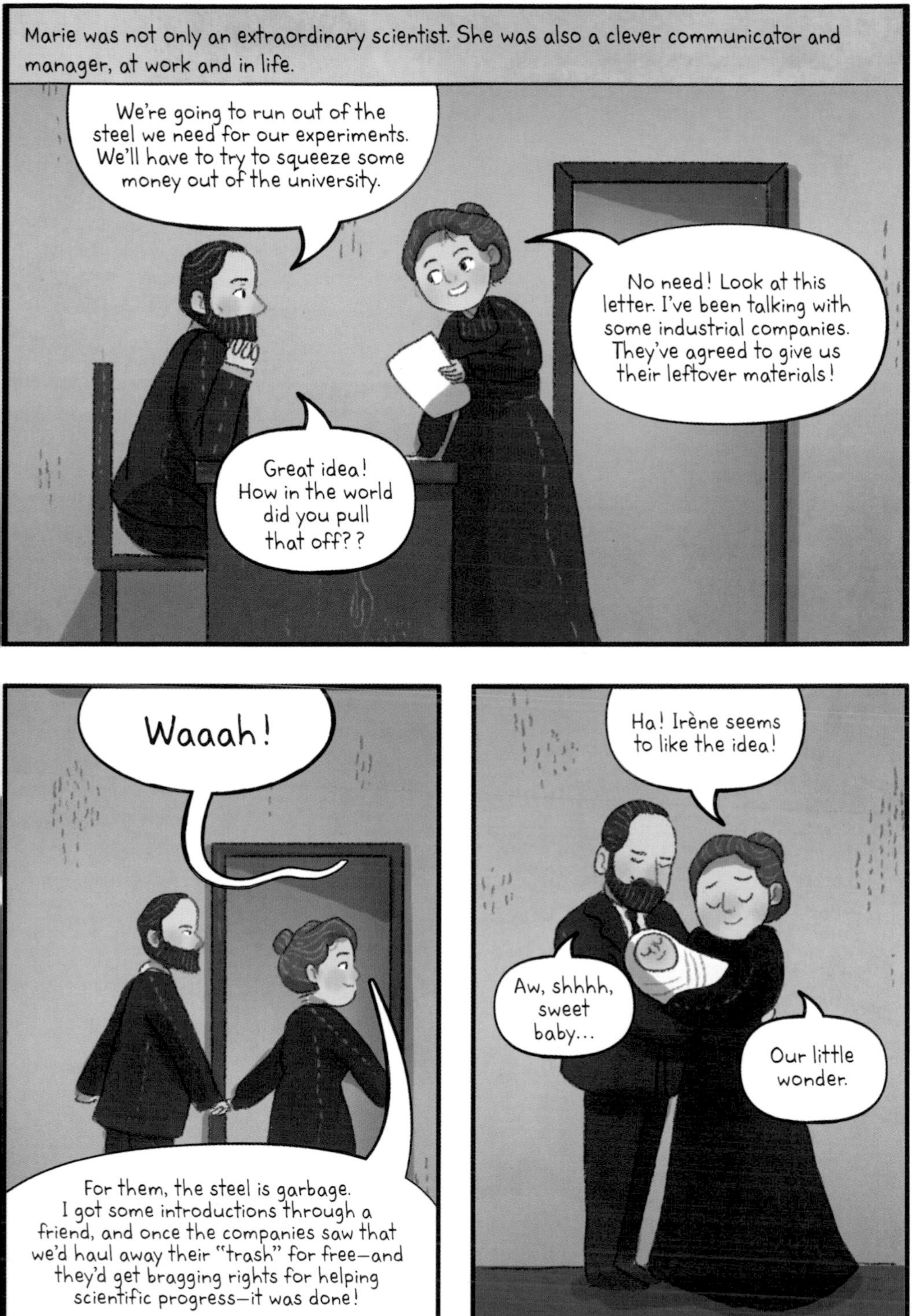
Marie was not only an extraordinary scientist. She was also a clever communicator and manager, at work and in life.
We're going to run out of the steel we need for our experiments. We'll have to try to squeeze some money out of the university.
No need! Look at this letter. I've been talking with some industrial companies. They've agreed to give us their leftover materials!
Great idea! How in the world did you pull that off??
Waaah!
For them, the steel is garbage. I got some introductions through a friend, and once the companies saw that we'd haul away their "trash" for free—and they'd get bragging rights for helping scientific progress—it was done!
Ha! Irène seems to like the idea!
Aw, shhhh, sweet baby...
Our little wonder.

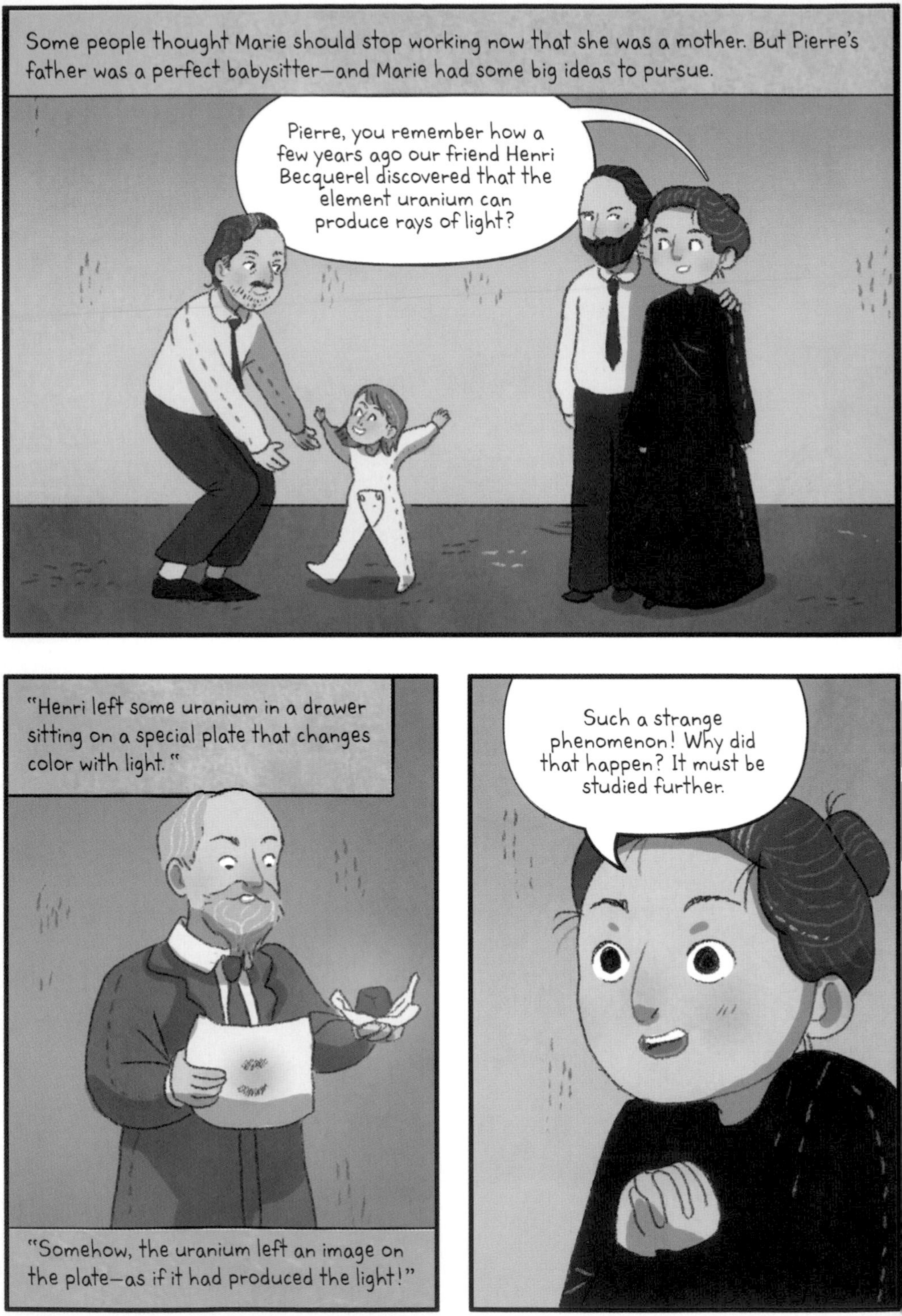
Some people thought Marie should stop working now that she was a mother. But Pierre's father was a perfect babysitter—and Marie had some big ideas to pursue.
Pierre, you remember how a few years ago our friend Henri Becquerel discovered that the element uranium can produce rays of light?
"Henri left some uranium in a drawer sitting on a special plate that changes color with light."
"Somehow, the uranium left an image on the plate—as if it had produced the light!"
Such a strange phenomenon! Why did that happen? It must be studied further.

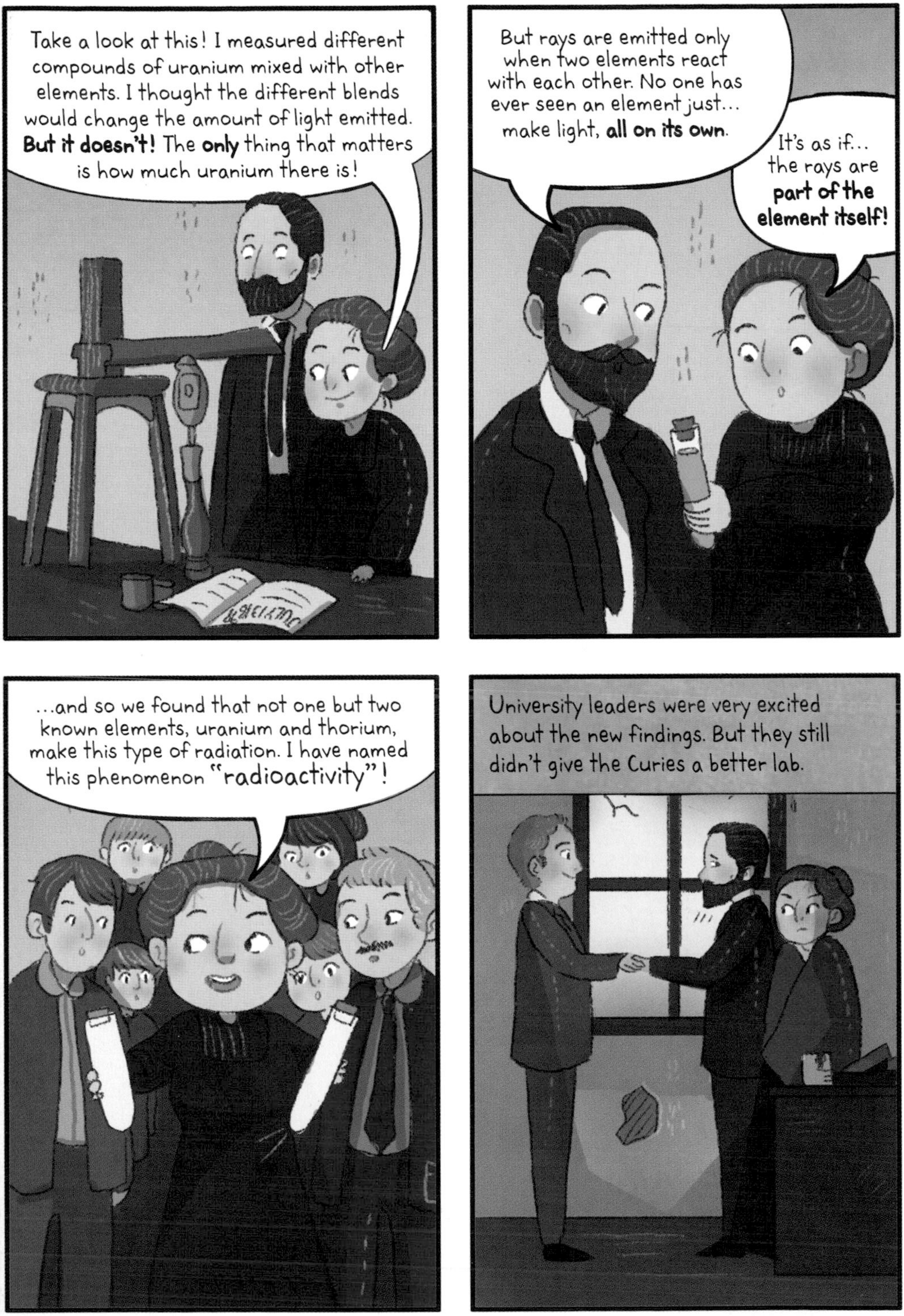
Take a look at this! I measured different compounds of uranium mixed with other elements. I thought the different blends would change the amount of light emitted. **But it doesn't!** The **only** thing that matters is how much uranium there is!
But rays are emitted only when two elements react with each other. No one has ever seen an element just... make light, **all on its own**.
It's as if... the rays are **part of the element itself!**
...and so we found that not one but two known elements, uranium and thorium, make this type of radiation. I have named this phenomenon "radioactivity"!
University leaders were very excited about the new findings. But they still didn't give the Curies a better lab.

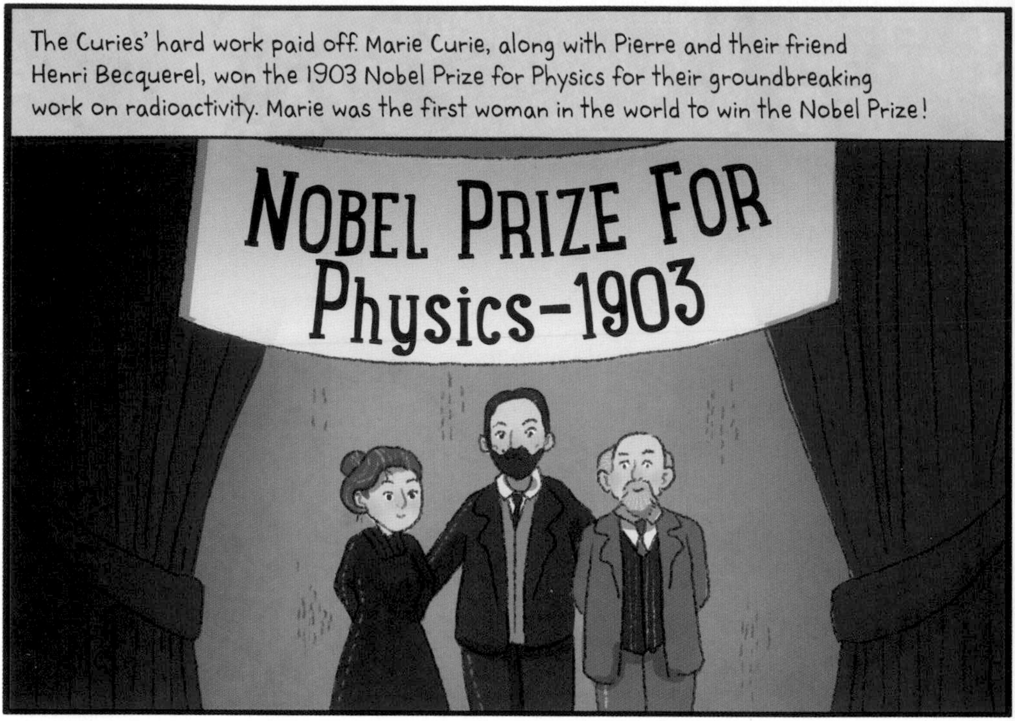
The Curies' hard work paid off. Marie Curie, along with Pierre and their friend Henri Becquerel, won the 1903 Nobel Prize for Physics for their groundbreaking work on radioactivity. Marie was the first woman in the world to win the Nobel Prize!
NOBEL PRIZE FOR Physics–1903

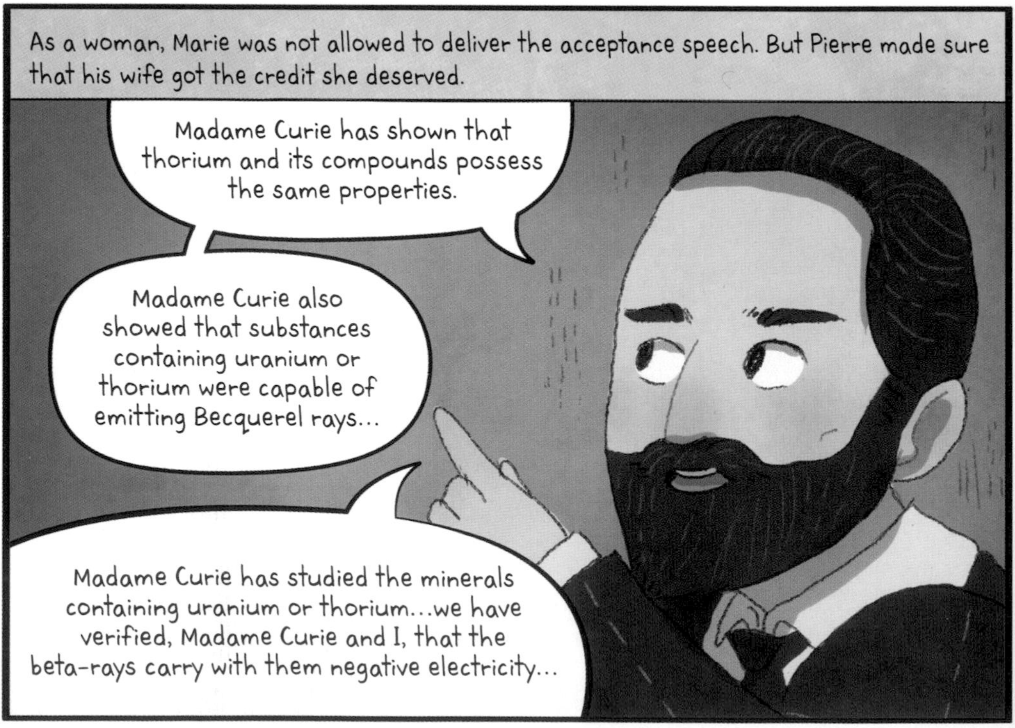
As a woman, Marie was not allowed to deliver the acceptance speech. But Pierre made sure that his wife got the credit she deserved.
Madame Curie has shown that thorium and its compounds possess the same properties.
Madame Curie also showed that substances containing uranium or thorium were capable of emitting Becquerel rays...
Madame Curie has studied the minerals containing uranium or thorium...we have verified, Madame Curie and I, that the beta-rays carry with them negative electricity...

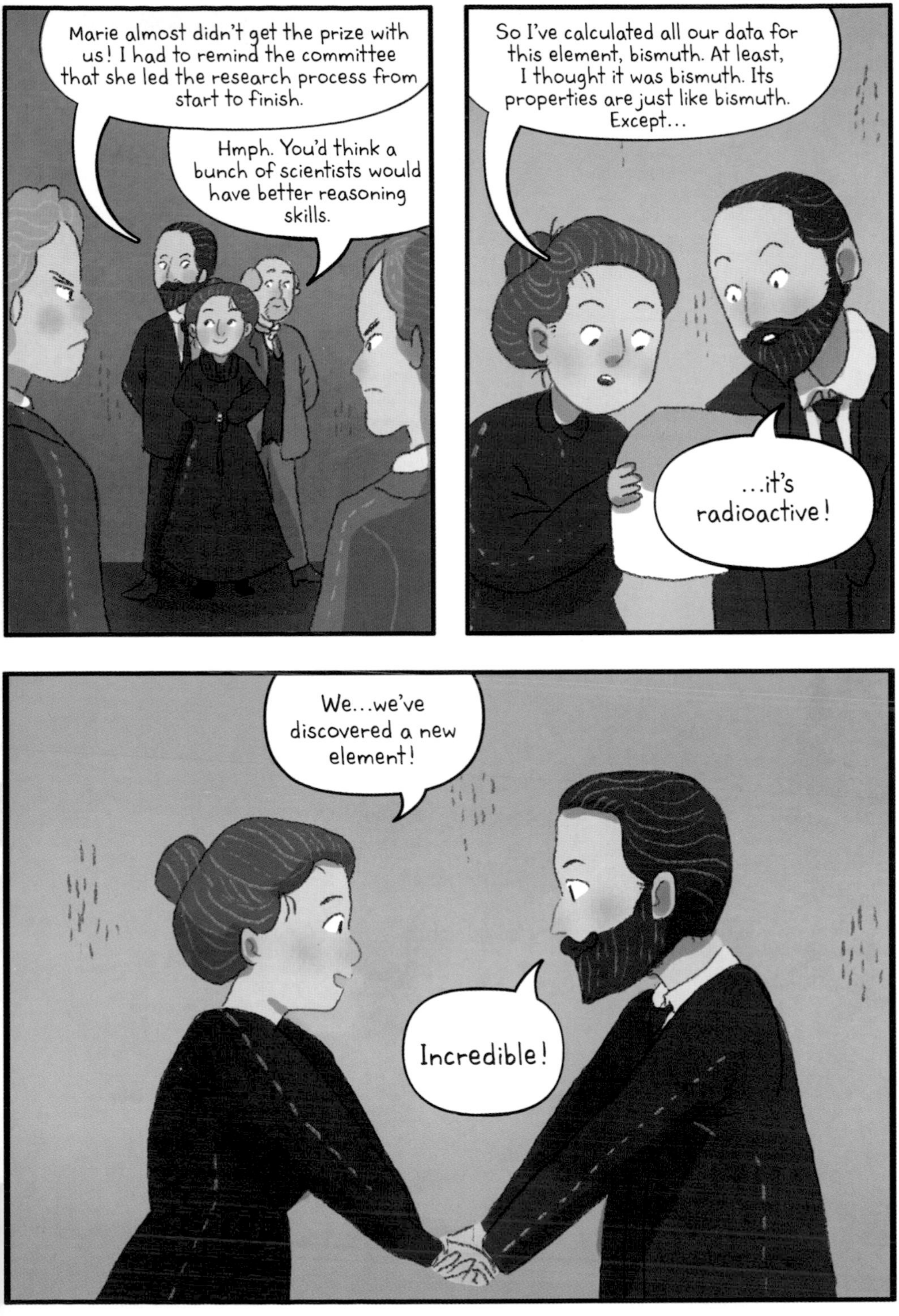
Marie almost didn't get the prize with us! I had to remind the committee that she led the research process from start to finish.
Hmph. You'd think a bunch of scientists would have better reasoning skills.
So I've calculated all our data for this element, bismuth. At least, I thought it was bismuth. Its properties are just like bismuth. Except...
...it's radioactive!
We...we've discovered a new element!
Incredible!

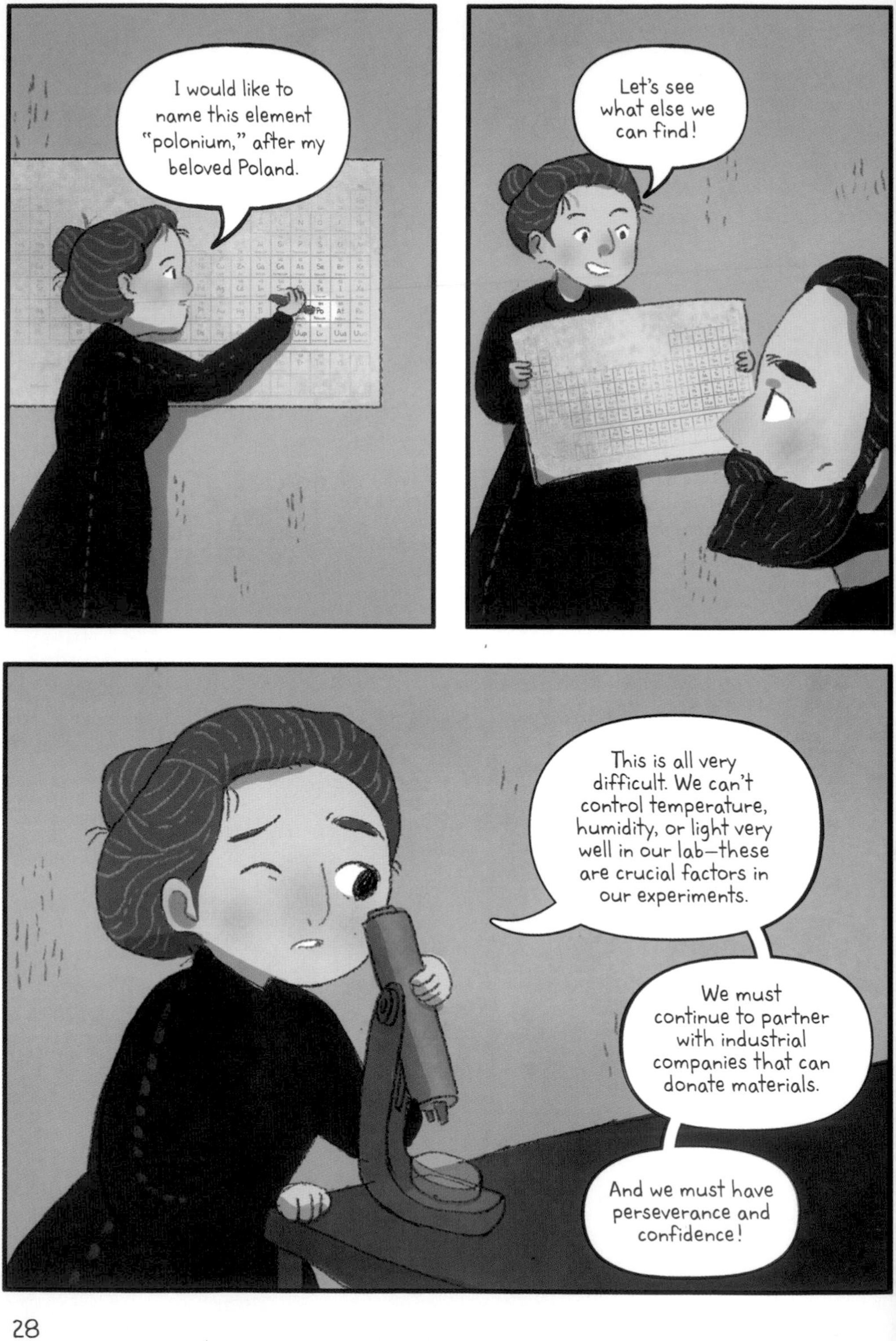
I would like to name this element "polonium," after my beloved Poland.
Let's see what else we can find!
This is all very difficult. We can't control temperature, humidity, or light very well in our lab—these are crucial factors in our experiments.
We must continue to partner with industrial companies that can donate materials.
And we must have perseverance and confidence!

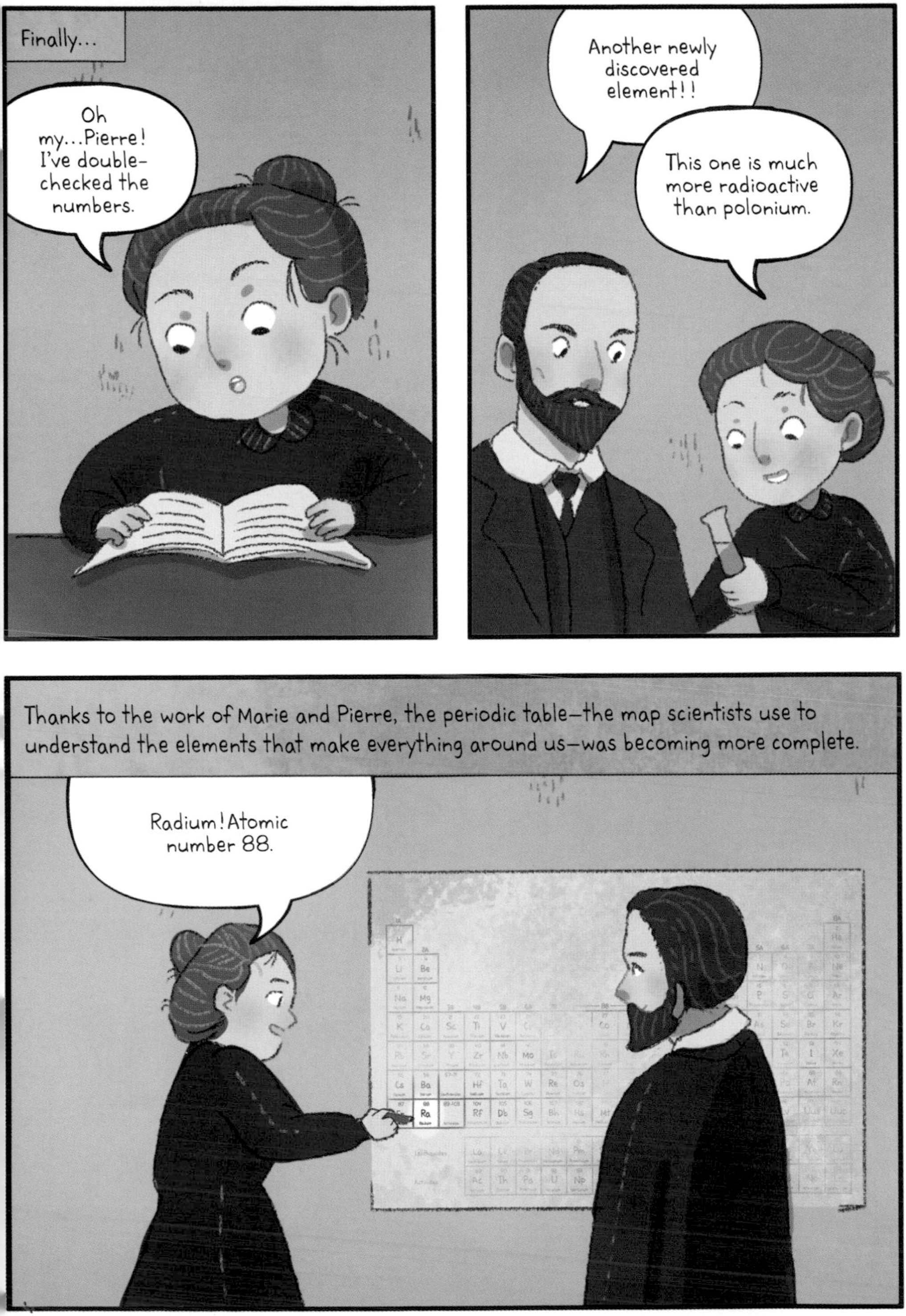
Finally...
Oh my...Pierre! I've double-checked the numbers.
Another newly discovered element!!
This one is much more radioactive than polonium.
Thanks to the work of Marie and Pierre, the periodic table—the map scientists use to understand the elements that make everything around us—was becoming more complete.
Radium! Atomic number 88.

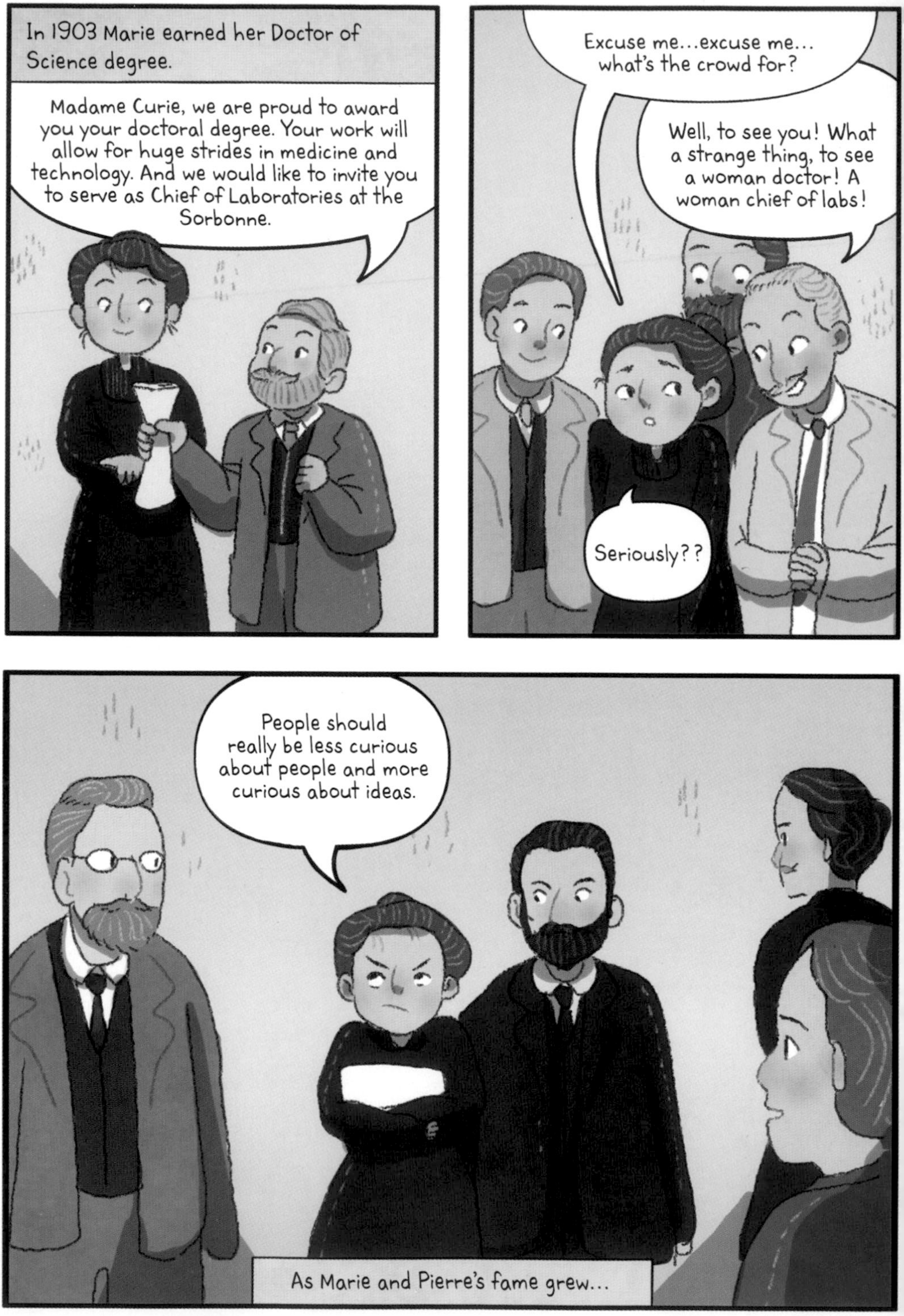
In 1903 Marie earned her Doctor of Science degree.
Madame Curie, we are proud to award you your doctoral degree. Your work will allow for huge strides in medicine and technology. And we would like to invite you to serve as Chief of Laboratories at the Sorbonne.
Excuse me...excuse me... what's the crowd for?
Well, to see you! What a strange thing, to see a woman doctor! A woman chief of labs!
Seriously??
People should really be less curious about people and more curious about ideas.
As Marie and Pierre's fame grew...

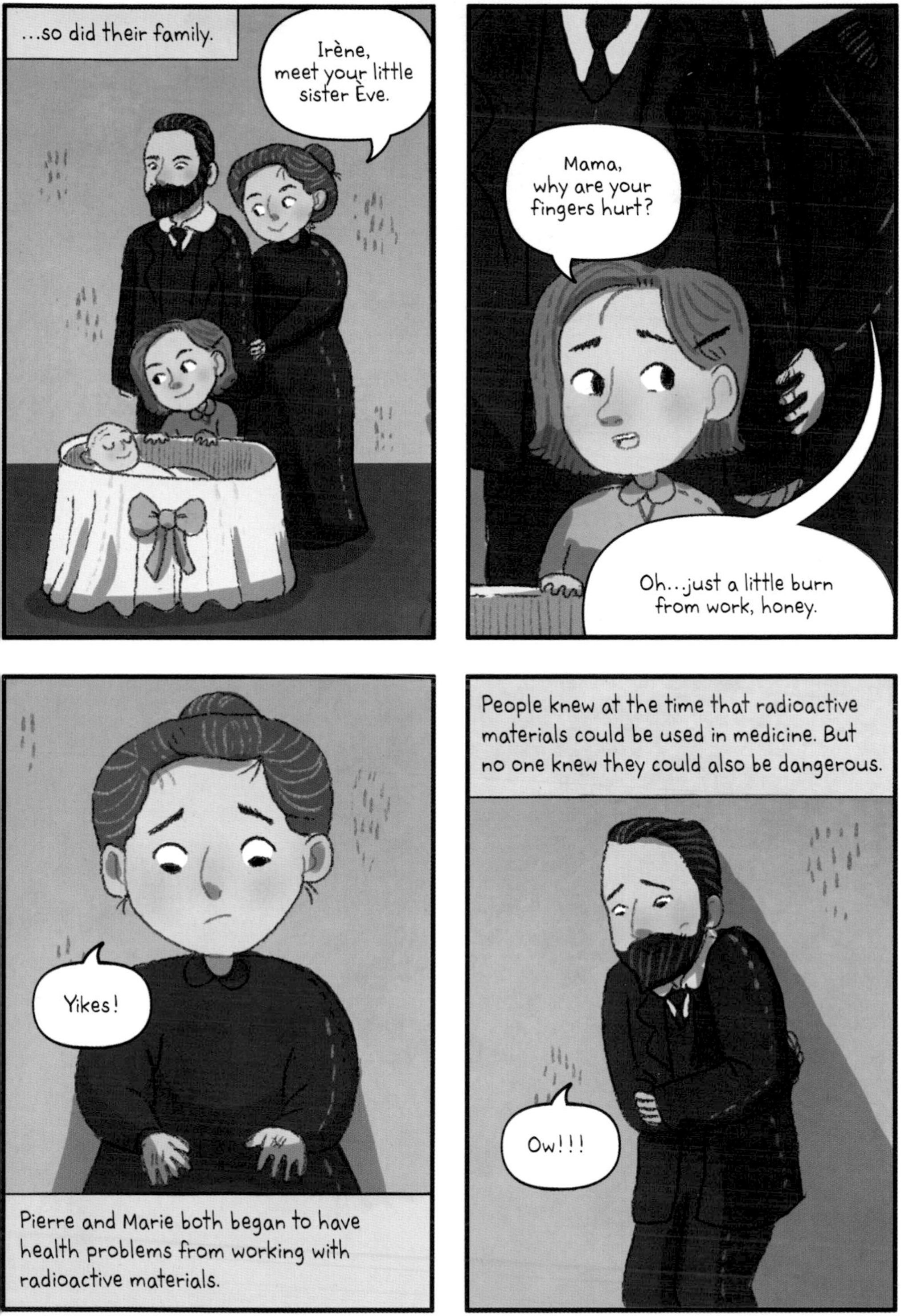

...so did their family.
Irène, meet your little sister Ève.
Mama, why are your fingers hurt?
Oh...just a little burn from work, honey.
Yikes!
Pierre and Marie both began to have health problems from working with radioactive materials.
People knew at the time that radioactive materials could be used in medicine. But no one knew they could also be dangerous.
Ow!!!

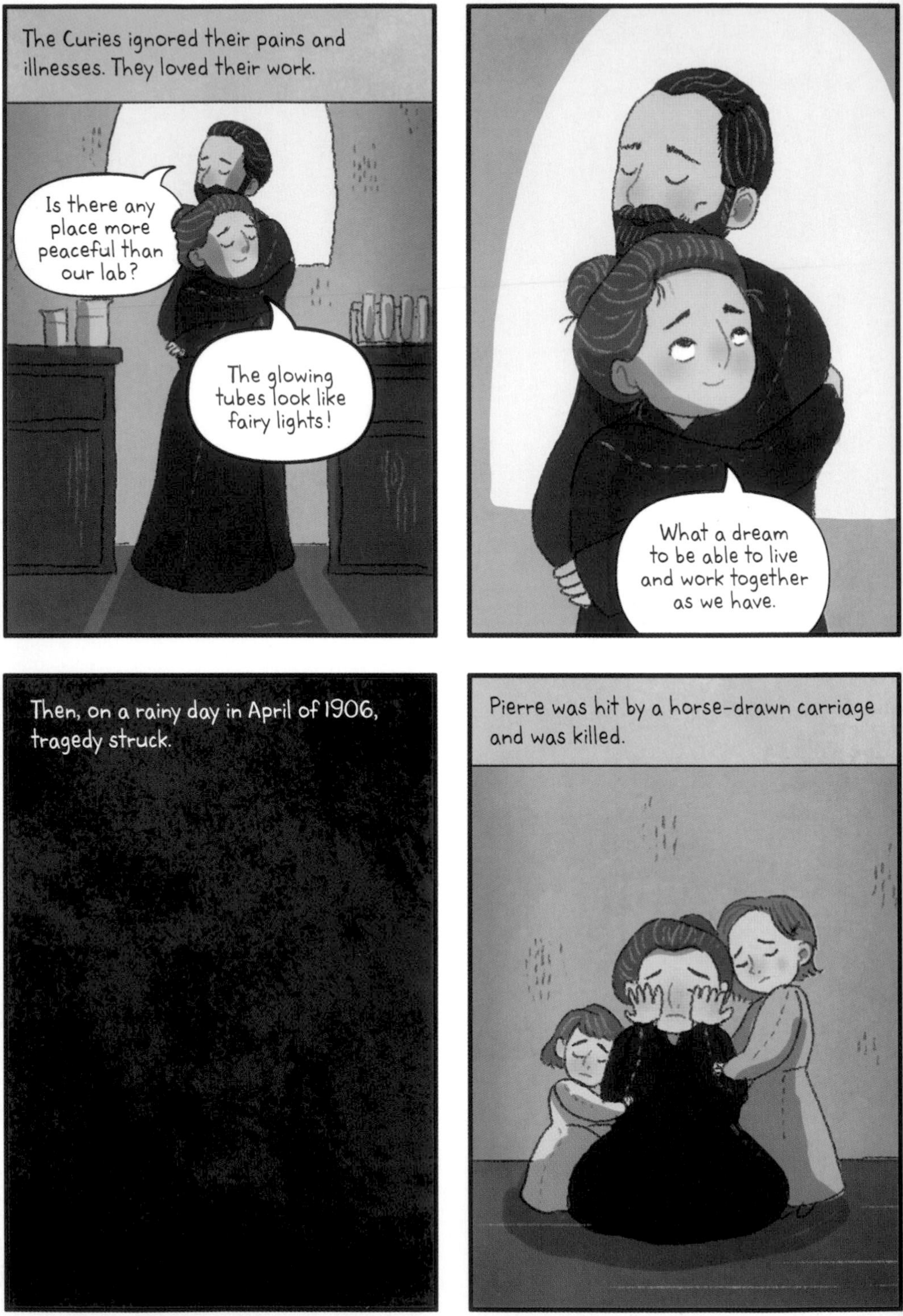
The Curies ignored their pains and illnesses. They loved their work.
Is there any place more peaceful than our lab?
The glowing tubes look like fairy lights!
What a dream to be able to live and work together as we have.
Then, on a rainy day in April of 1906, tragedy struck.
Pierre was hit by a horse-drawn carriage and was killed.

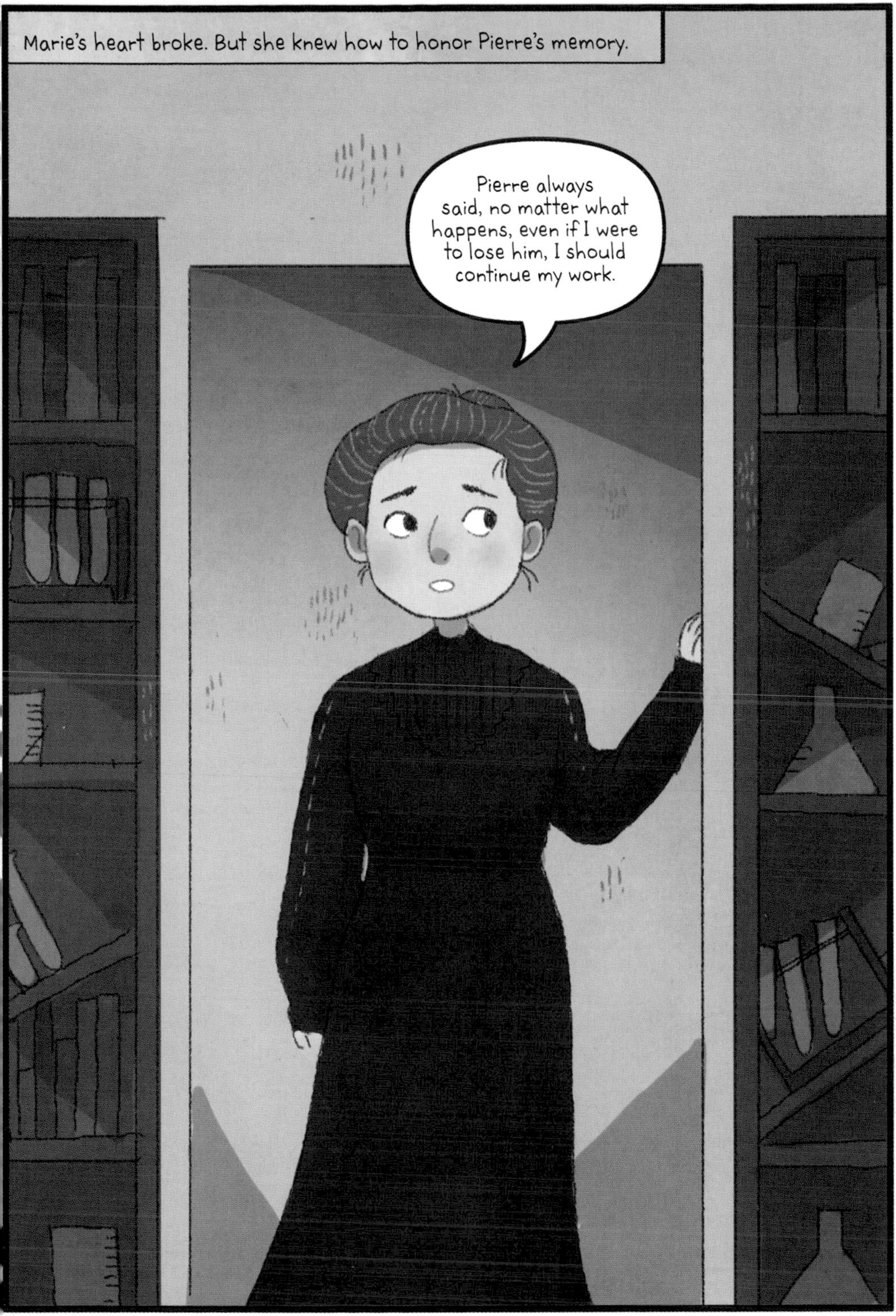
Marie's heart broke. But she knew how to honor Pierre's memory.
Pierre always said, no matter what happens, even if I were to lose him, I should continue my work.

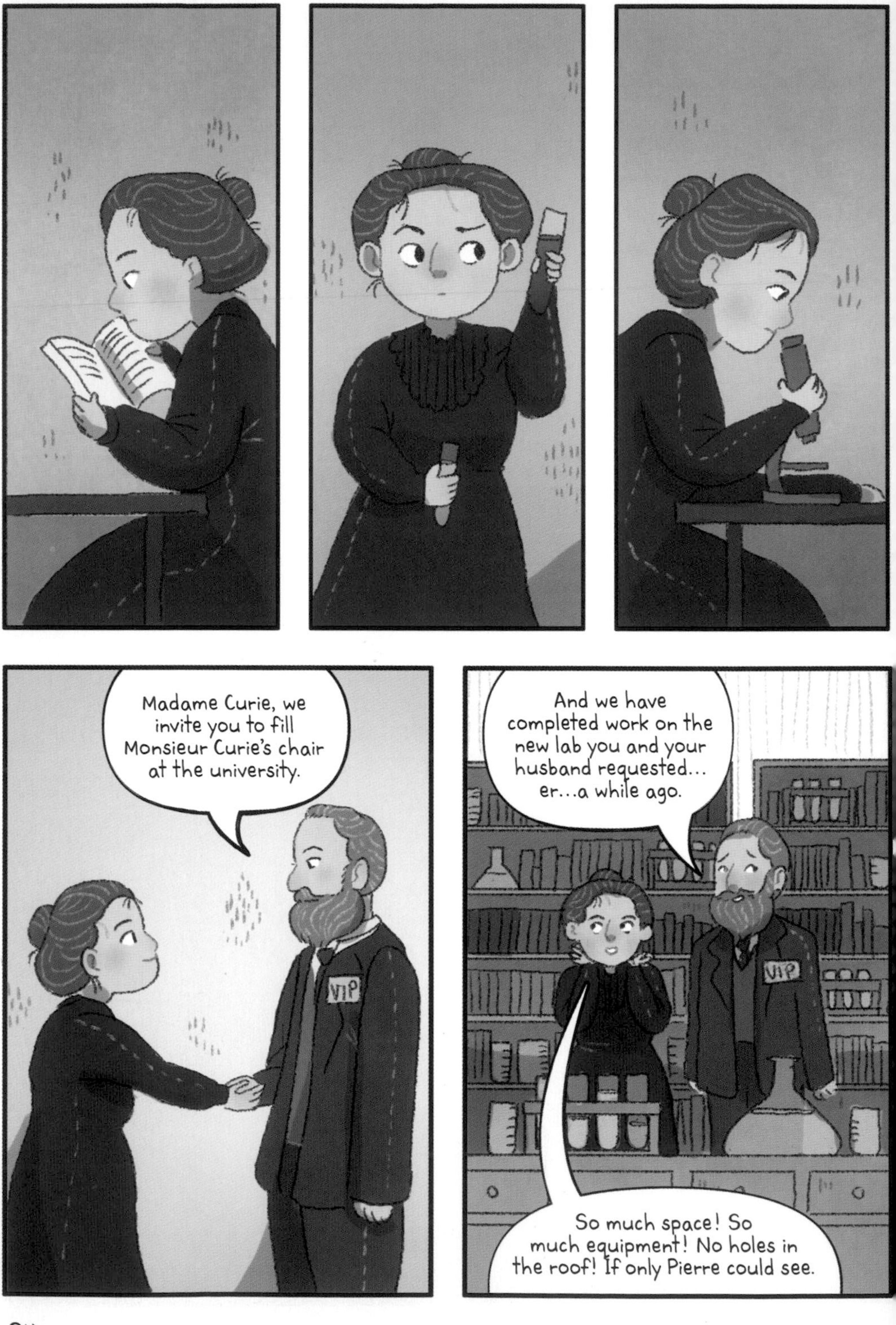
Madame Curie, we invite you to fill Monsieur Curie's chair at the university.
And we have completed work on the new lab you and your husband requested... er...a while ago.
VIP
VIP
So much space! So much equipment! No holes in the roof! If only Pierre could see.

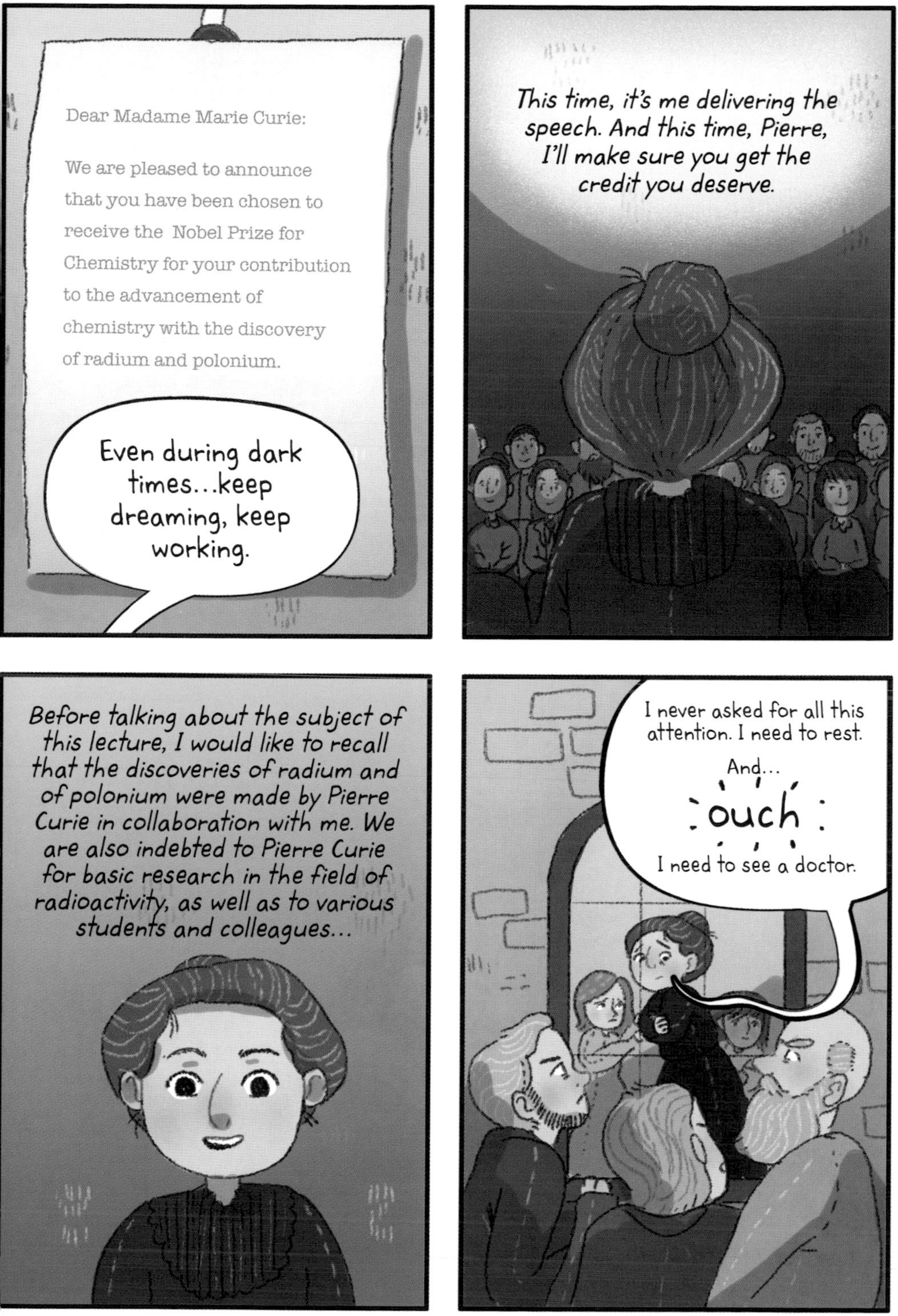
Dear Madame Marie Curie:
We are pleased to announce that you have been chosen to receive the Nobel Prize for Chemistry for your contribution to the advancement of chemistry with the discovery of radium and polonium.
Even during dark times...keep dreaming, keep working.
This time, it's me delivering the speech. And this time, Pierre, I'll make sure you get the credit you deserve.
Before talking about the subject of this lecture, I would like to recall that the discoveries of radium and of polonium were made by Pierre Curie in collaboration with me. We are also indebted to Pierre Curie for basic research in the field of radioactivity, as well as to various students and colleagues...
I never asked for all this attention. I need to rest.
And...
ouch
I need to see a doctor.

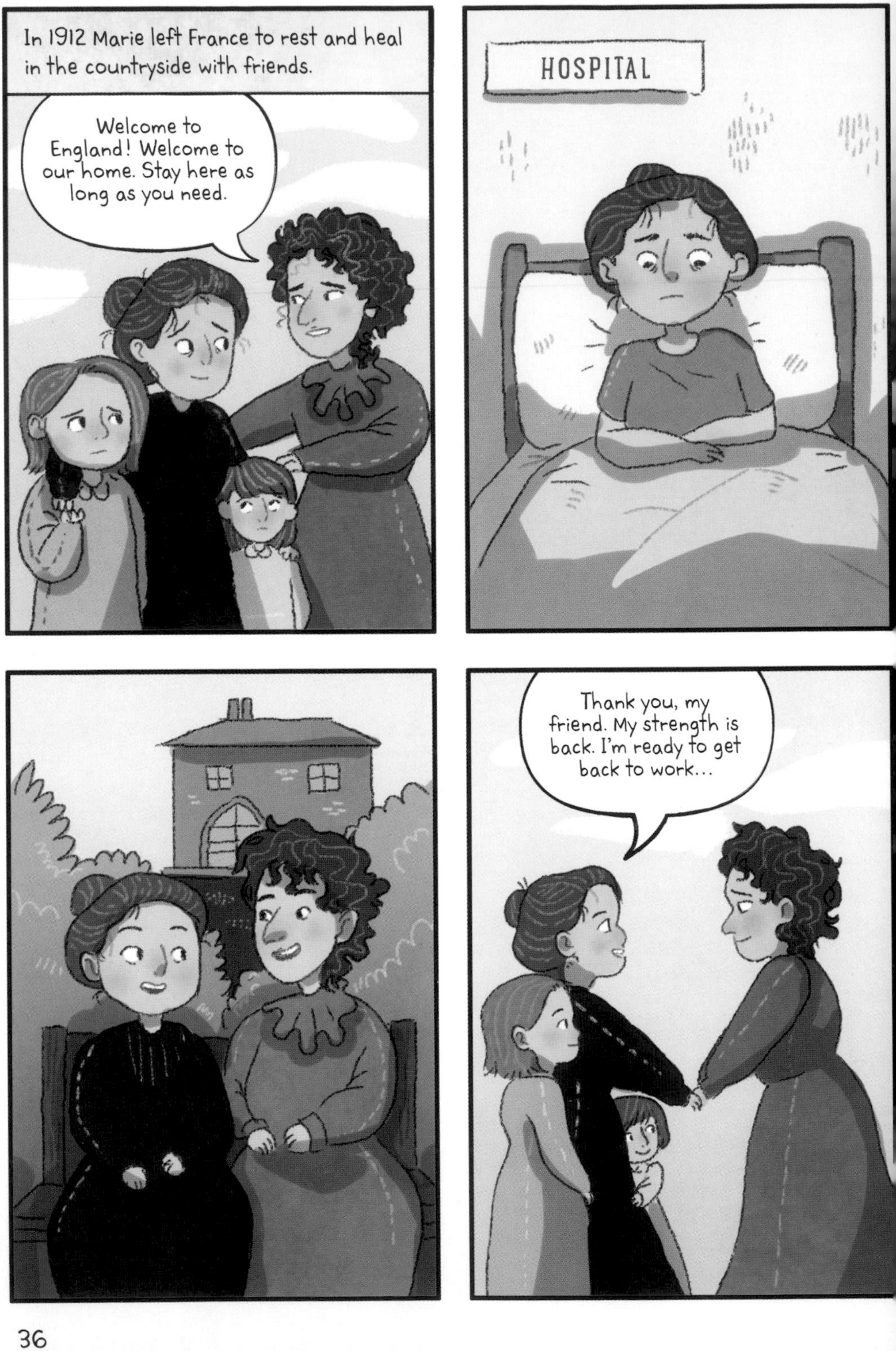
In 1912 Marie left France to rest and heal in the countryside with friends.
Welcome to England! Welcome to our home. Stay here as long as you need.
HOSPITAL
Thank you, my friend. My strength is back. I'm ready to get back to work...

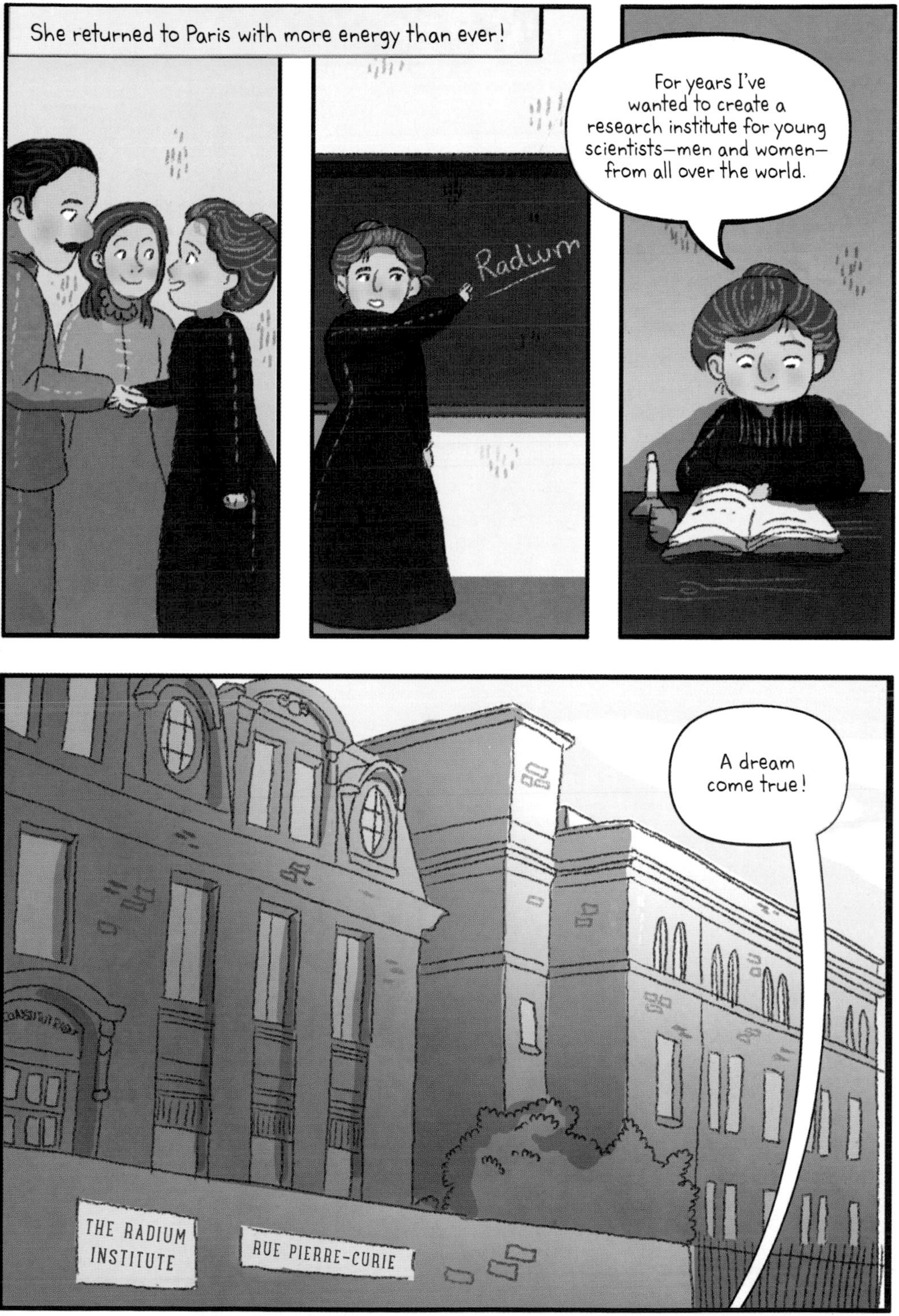
She returned to Paris with more energy than ever!
Radium
For years I've wanted to create a research institute for young scientists—men and women—from all over the world.
THE RADIUM INSTITUTE
RUE PIERRE-CURIE
A dream come true!

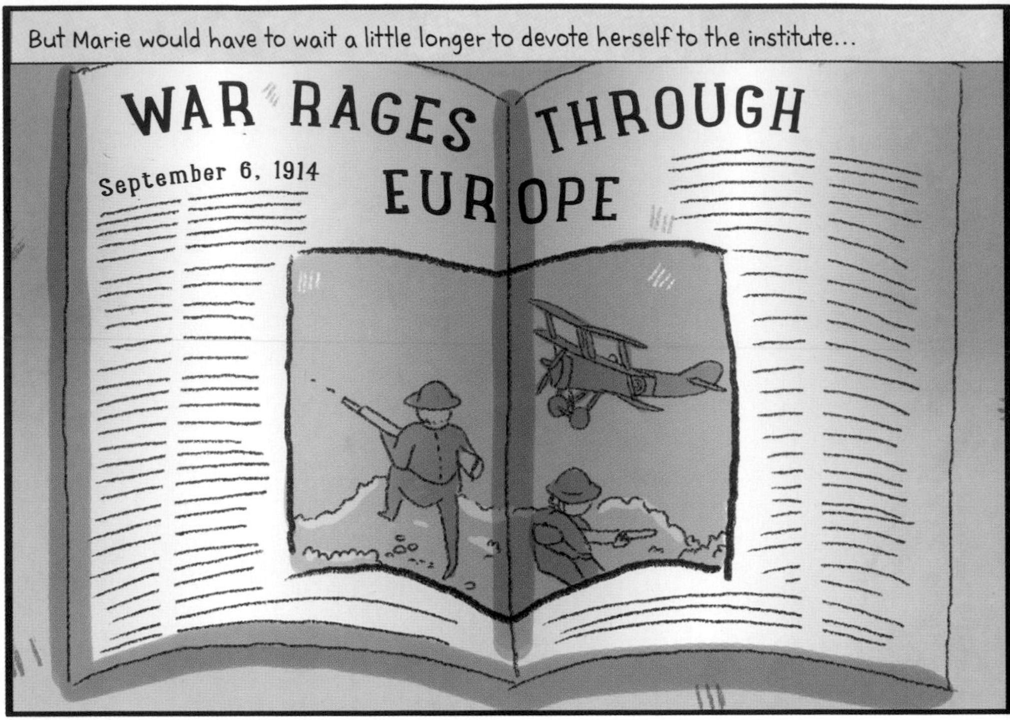
But Marie would have to wait a little longer to devote herself to the institute...
WAR RAGES THROUGH EUROPE
September 6, 1914

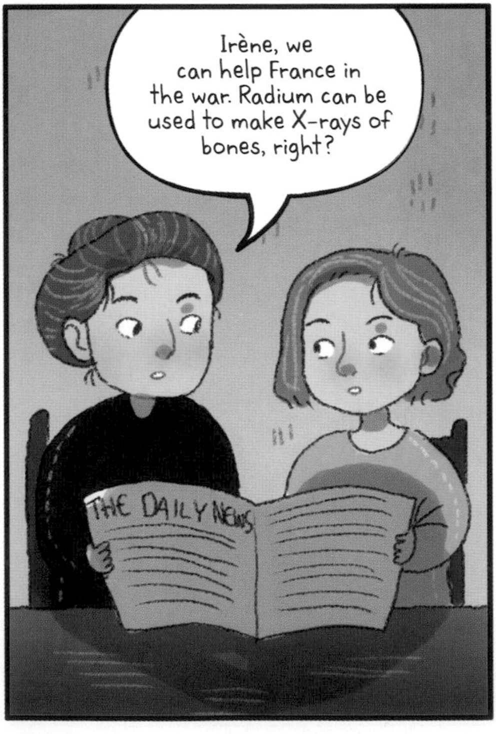
Irène, we can help France in the war. Radium can be used to make X-rays of bones, right?
THE DAILY NEWS

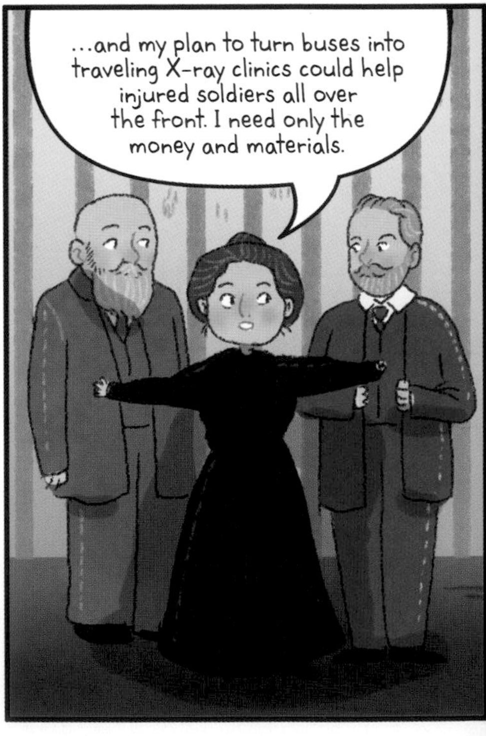
...and my plan to turn buses into traveling X-ray clinics could help injured soldiers all over the front. I need only the money and materials.

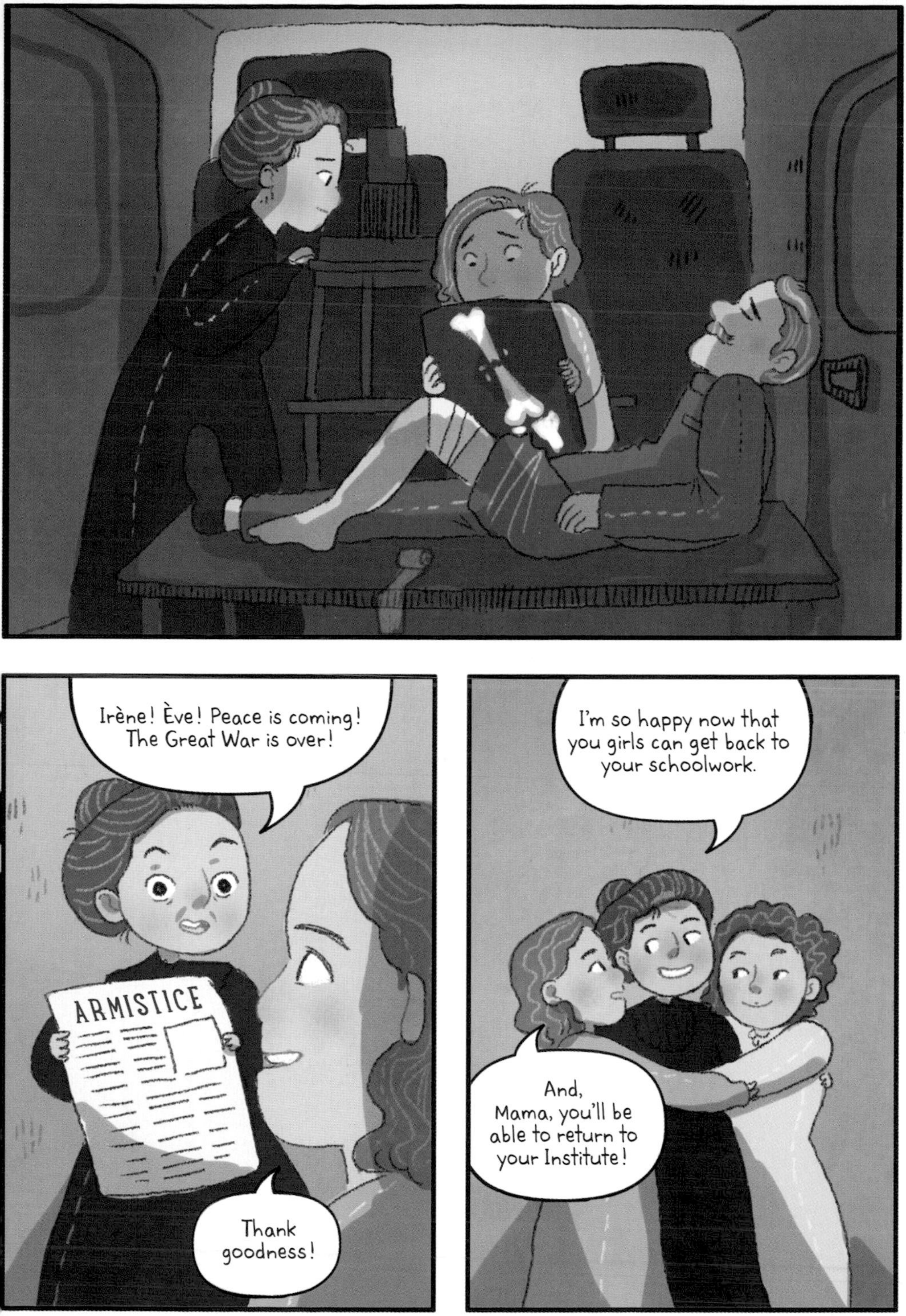
Irène! Ève! Peace is coming! The Great War is over!
ARMISTICE
Thank goodness!
I'm so happy now that you girls can get back to your schoolwork.
And, Mama, you'll be able to return to your Institute!

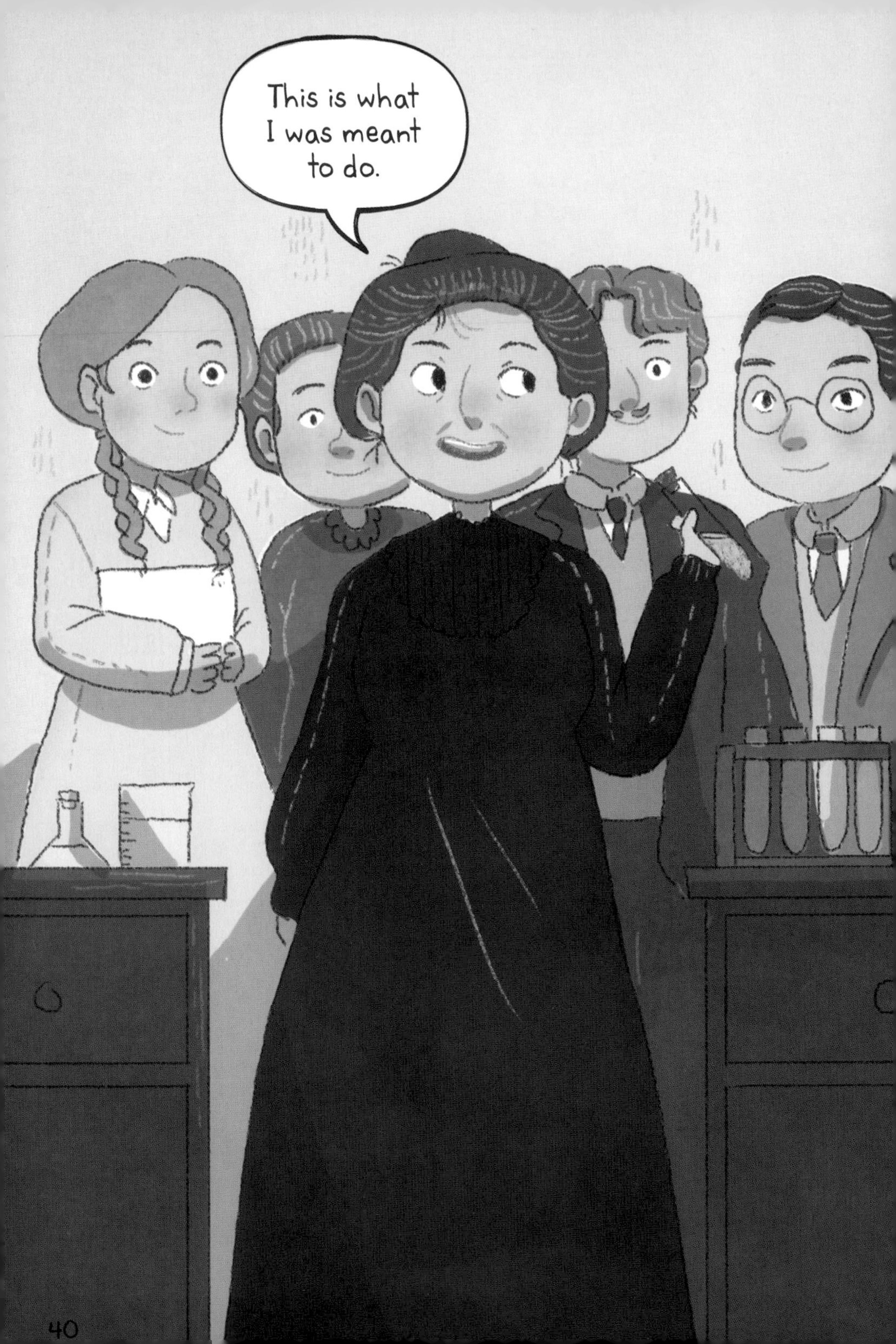
This is what I was meant to do.

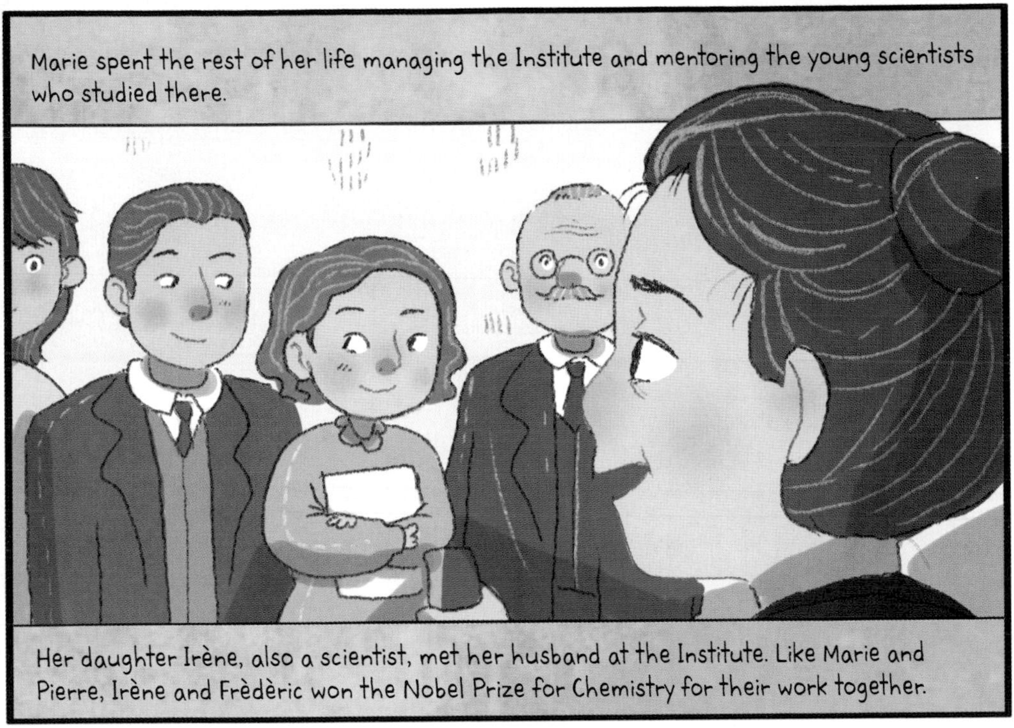
Marie spent the rest of her life managing the Institute and mentoring the young scientists who studied there.
Her daughter Irène, also a scientist, met her husband at the Institute. Like Marie and Pierre, Irène and Frèdèric won the Nobel Prize for Chemistry for their work together.

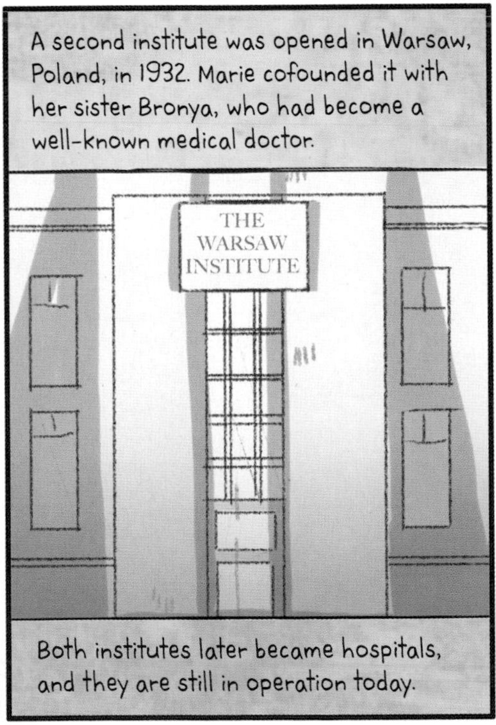
A second institute was opened in Warsaw, Poland, in 1932. Marie cofounded it with her sister Bronya, who had become a well-known medical doctor.
THE WARSAW INSTITUTE
Both institutes later became hospitals, and they are still in operation today.

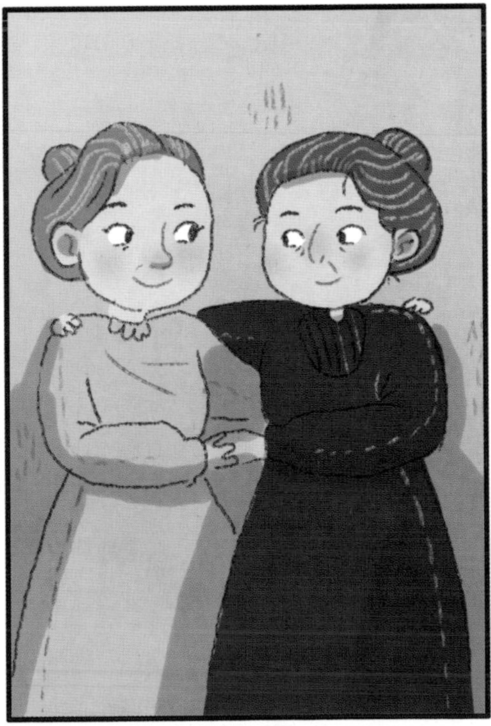

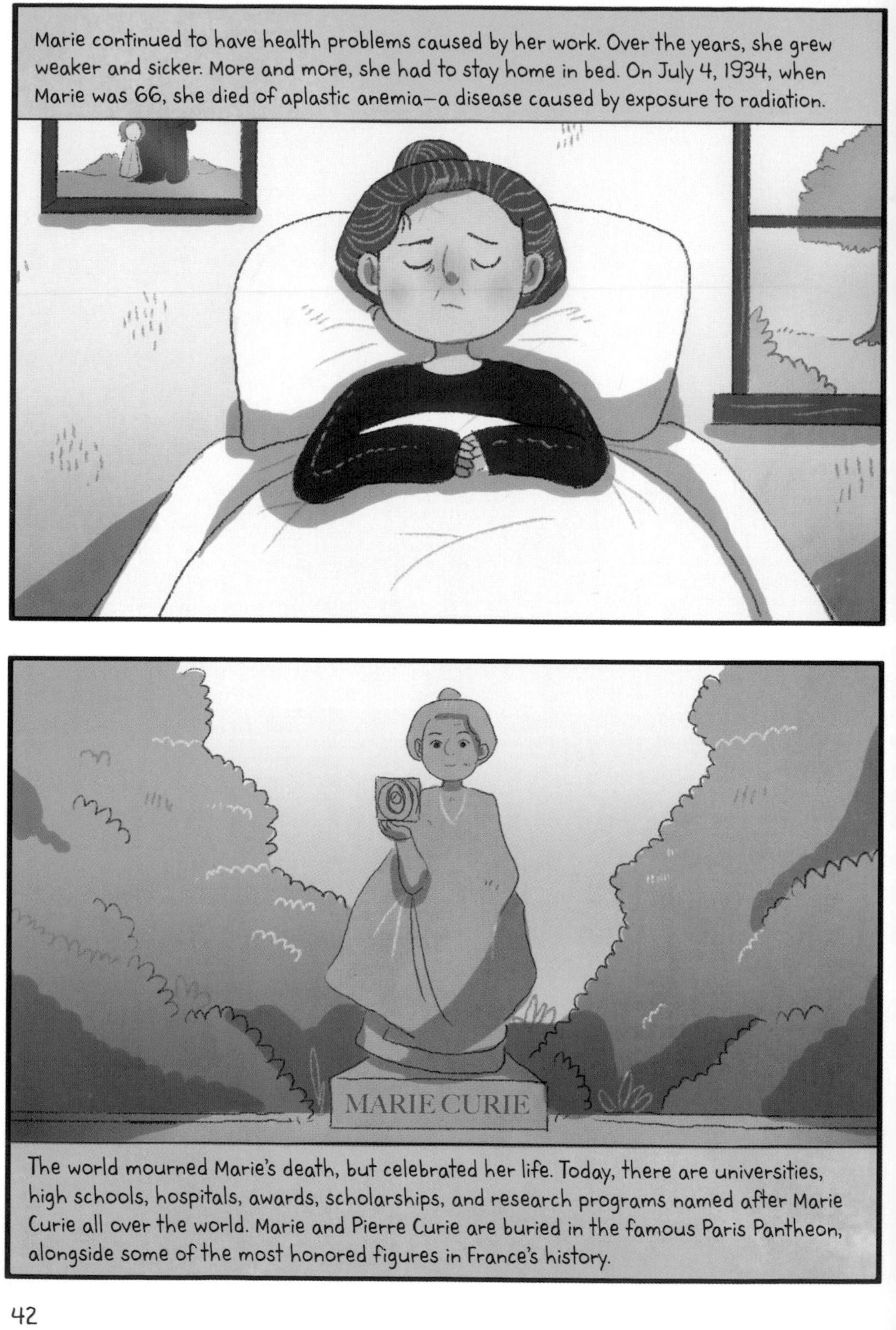
Marie continued to have health problems caused by her work. Over the years, she grew weaker and sicker. More and more, she had to stay home in bed. On July 4, 1934, when Marie was 66, she died of aplastic anemia—a disease caused by exposure to radiation.
MARIE CURIE
The world mourned Marie's death, but celebrated her life. Today, there are universities, high schools, hospitals, awards, scholarships, and research programs named after Marie Curie all over the world. Marie and Pierre Curie are buried in the famous Paris Pantheon, alongside some of the most honored figures in France's history.

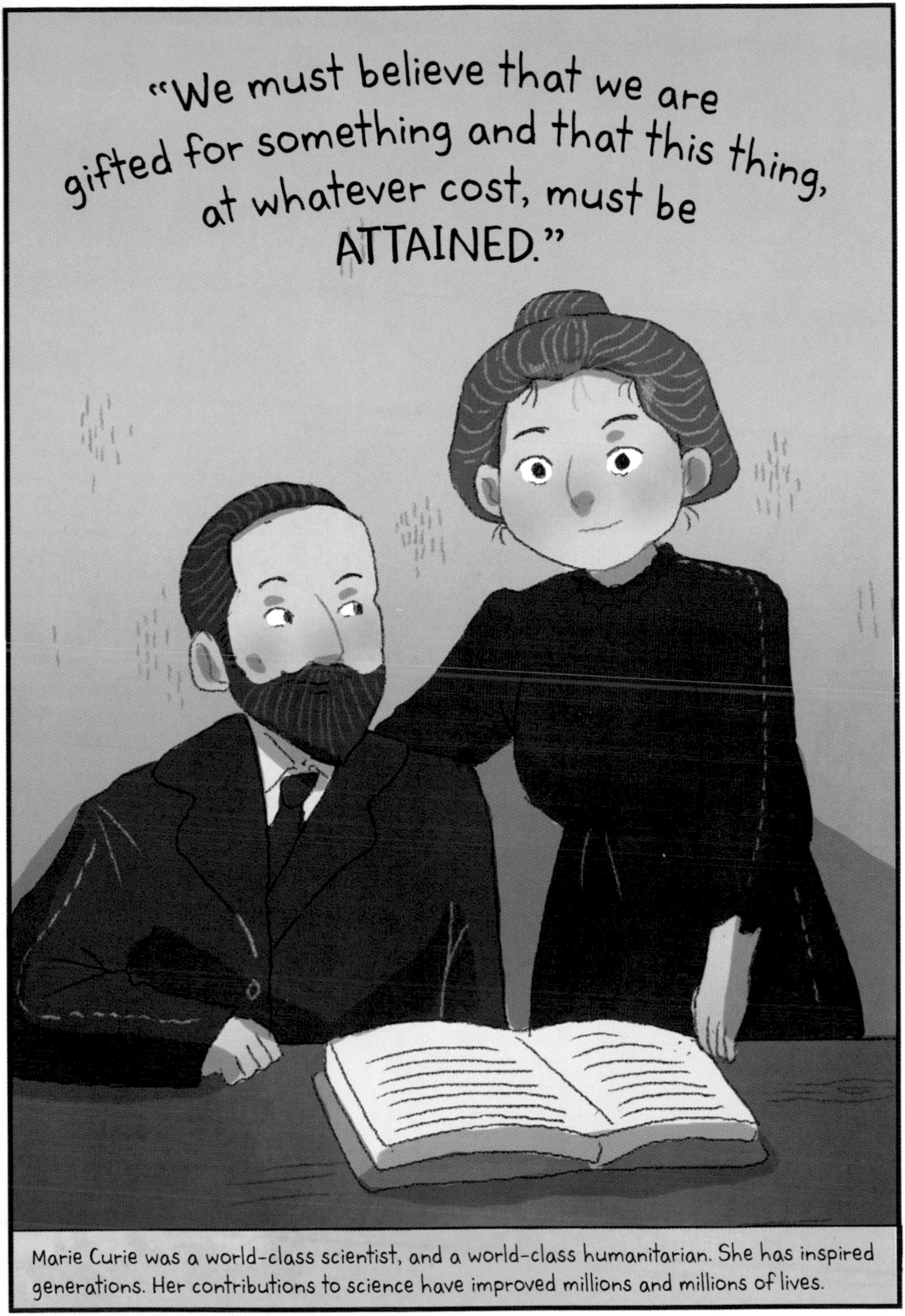
"We must believe that we are gifted for something and that this thing, at whatever cost, must be ATTAINED."
Marie Curie was a world-class scientist, and a world-class humanitarian. She has inspired generations. Her contributions to science have improved millions and millions of lives.

And it all started when she was a curious kid.

Maybe just like you!

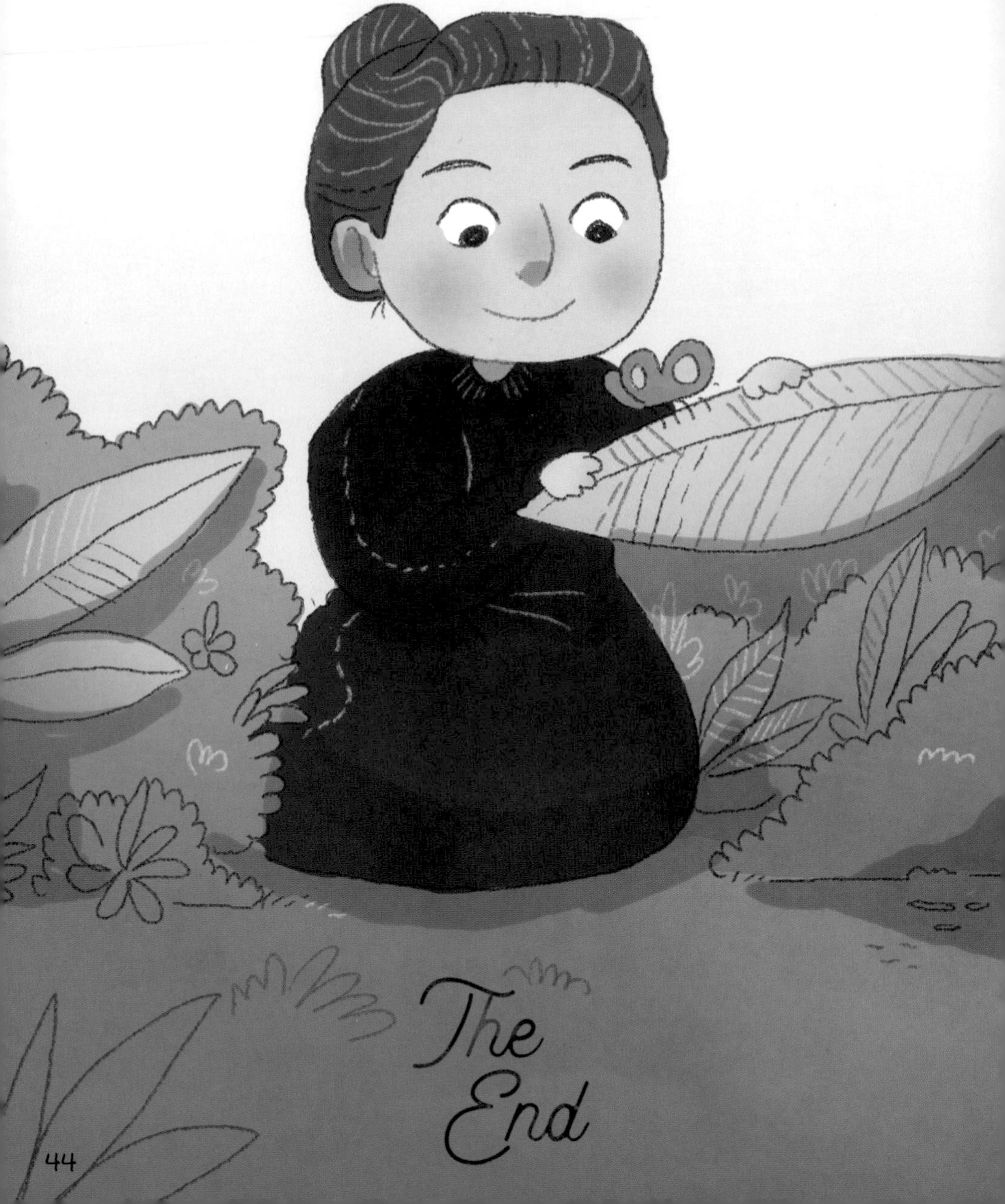

The End

Kaara Kallen is a writer, editor, teacher, learner, and activist. When she is not writing about inspiring scientist-humanitarians, she is working to make the world safer for wildlife and people. She lives in Chicago with her husband, their daughter, and one or more cats.

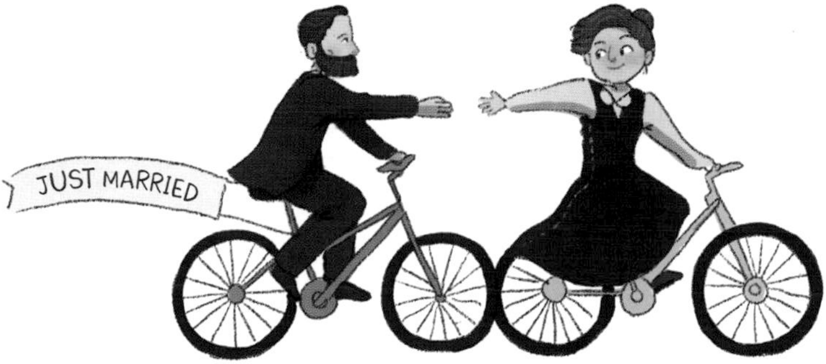
JUST MARRIED

Rosie Baker was lucky enough to grow up in Dorset, England, surrounded by nature and a creative family. She began her artistic career using sticks, mud, and crayons, developing a passion for using color to create bright and lively pictures. Later on she discovered a love of comic books and digital artwork and has since been having the time of her life working on books such as this one! Currently Rosie enjoys living by the sea and drawing every day surrounded by her many plants.

Also available:

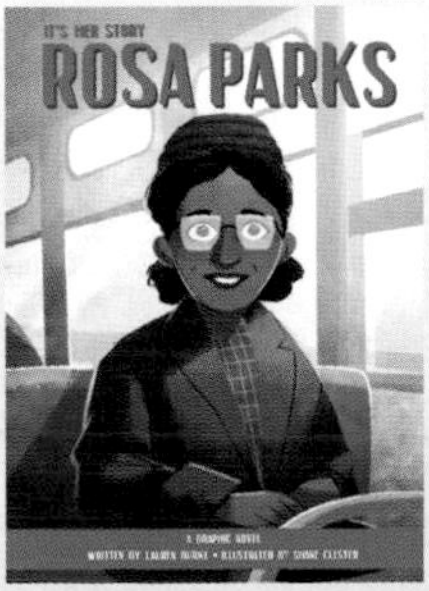
ROSA PARKS

PERIODIC TABLE

IA								
1 **H** Hydrogen	**2A**							
3 **Li** Lithium	4 **Be** Beryllium							
11 **Na** Sodium	12 **Mg** Magnesium	**3B**	**4B**	**5B**	**6B**	**7B**		**8B**
19 **K** Potassium	20 **Ca** Calcium	21 **Sc** Scandium	22 **Ti** Titanium	23 **V** Vanadium	24 **Cr** Chromium	25 **Mn** Manganese	26 **Fe** Iron	27 **Co** Cobalt
37 **Rb** Rubidium	38 **Sr** Strontium	39 **Y** Yttrium	40 **Zr** Zirconium	41 **Nb** Niobium	42 **Mo** Molybdenum	43 **Tc** Technetium	44 **Ru** Ruthenium	45 **Rh** Rhodium
55 **Cs** Cesium	56 **Ba** Barium	57-71 Lanthanides	72 **Hf** Hafnium	73 **Ta** Tantalum	74 **W** Tungsten	75 **Re** Rhenium	76 **Os** Osmium	77 **Ir** Iridium
87 **Fr** Francium	88 **Ra** Radium	89-103 Actinides	104 **Rf** Rutherfordium	105 **Db** Dubnium	106 **Sg** Seaborgium	107 **Bh** Bohrium	108 **Hs** Hassium	109 **Mt** Meitnerium

Lanthanides	57 **La** Lanthanum	58 **Ce** Cerium	59 **Pr** Praseodymium	60 **Nd** Neodymium	61 **Pm** Promethium	62 **Sm** Samarium
Actinides	89 **Ac** Actinium	90 **Th** Thorium	91 **Pa** Protactinium	92 **U** Uranium	93 **Np** Neptunium	94 **Pu** Plutonium